International English

Workbook 2

International English

Workbook 2

Lydia Kellas
Peter Lucantoni

HODDER EDUCATION
AN HACHETTE UK COMPANY

Acknowledgements

The Publishers would like to thank the following for permission to reproduce copyright material:

p.15 Pan pipes myth from *Myths and Legends,* retold by Anthony Horowitz (Kingfisher, 1991); **p.29** Enid Blyton, extract from *The Ring O' Bells Mystery* (Mulberry Editions/HarperCollins Publishers, 1992); **p.42** text about the sounds of London (adapted) from *http://www.folger.edu/template.cfm?cid=2055 Accessed 07.31.08,* copyright © Folger Shakespeare Library; **p.58** text about the TV series *Lost* (adapted) from *www.wikipedia.org/w/index.php?title=Lost_%28TV_series%29&printable=yes* (08/02/2008); **p.76** extract about oil (adapted) from *http://en.wikipedia.org/wiki/Oil* (24.08.08); **p.79** text and bar chart about urban competitiveness (adapted) from *The Economist* (August 16th 2008); **p.90** Arkady Leokum, text about Neanderthal man from *Still More Tell Me Why* (Hamlyn Children's Books, 1982); **pp.95–96** Dylan Thomas, 'The Song of the Mischievous Dog' from *The Oxford Book of Children's Poetry* (Oxford University Press, 2007); **p.104** predictions about society (adapted) from *The World Guide 2001/2002* (New Internationalist Publications, 2001).

Every effort has been made to trace all copyright holders, but if any have been inadvertently overlooked the Publishers will be pleased to make the necessary arrangements at the first opportunity.

Hachette UK's policy is to use papers that are natural, renewable and recyclable products and made from wood grown in sustainable forests. The logging and manufacturing processes are expected to conform to the environmental regulations of the country of origin.

Orders: please contact Bookpoint Ltd, 130 Milton Park, Abingdon, Oxon OX14 4SB.
Telephone: (44) 01235 827720. Fax: (44) 01235 400454. Lines are open 9.00–5.00, Monday to Saturday, with a 24-hour message answering service. Visit our website at www.hoddereducation.co.uk.

© Lydia Kellas and Peter Lucantoni 2009
First published in 2009 by
Hodder Education, an Hachette UK Company,
338 Euston Road
London NW1 3BH

Impression number   5
Year   2015   2014

Cover photo © David Muench/Stone/Getty Images
Illustrations by Robert Hitchens Design
Typeset in 12.5/15.5 pt Garamond by Macmillan Publishing Solutions
Printed and bound by CPI Group (UK) Ltd, Croydon, CR0 4YY

A catalogue record for this title is available from the British Library

ISBN 978 0 340 95945 9

Contents

Vocabulary

1 Find the names of the characters and match them to each of the pictures. Don't worry about the 'Words' spaces yet.

King a   Hlakanyana b   Arthur a
Merlin   the wizard c

	a)	b)	c)
Name			
Words	i) *sword* ii) *crown*	i) *cunning* ii) *clever*	i) *spell* ii) *wand*

2 Now connect two words to each of the characters above.

> wand   sword
>
> cunning   crown
>
> spell   clever

3 The letters of each word have been mixed up. Put the letters into the correct order and write the word next to its meaning.
   a) r g a m n t u e   *argument*   a heated discussion
   b) e p e t s m h a r o   *atmosphere*   the air around us
   c) m d a t o m c i c o o a n   *accomodation*   a place to stay
   d) e a l n s a y   *analyse*   to find out exactly
   e) m s a t n s e s s e   *assessment*   test
   f) t g l u a h o h   *although*   even if
   g) l a c t l y a u   *actually*   real and clear
   h) l s i s n y a a   *analysis*   the noun of (d)

4 a) Write the word which is opposite in meaning to the following:

> arrive – leave

i) friendly _unfriendly_   vi) methodical _unmethodical_

ii) large _small_   vii) uniform _multiform_

iii) small _large_   viii) old _new/young_

iv) disciplined _agitation_   ix) whiteboards _blackboards_

v) academic _unacademic_   x) formal _informal_

b) Now write a sentence explaining the difference between the two words.

> arrive/leave – Arrive means that you get to a place, leave means that you go away.

i) _Friendly – unfriendly – Friendly means being kind and gentle to others, unfriendly means being mean and awful to others._

ii) _Large means something that is big._
Small means something that is a little tiny.

iii) _" " " " " " " " " " "_
Large " " " " " " big.

iv) _Disciplined means forceing a system/order on others_
Agitation " out of control exitment

v) _Academic is a kind of school that have a high education_
Unacademic is a kind of school that doesn't have a high education

vi) _Disciplined means to obey the rules._
Agitation means to disobey the rules.

vii) _Uniform mans some different members wearing the same cl_
Multiform means many different shaps and clother

viii) _Old maeans something/somebody that is aged and have strayed for le_
New/young means something/somebody that is rejuvenated.

ix) _Whiteboards are a flat boards that we write with markers on_
Blackboards are a flat boords that we write with chalk an

x) _Formal means officialy correct._
Informal " free of ceremony.

Grammar

1 Read the text about Frodo Baggins and find and correct the **ten** mistakes with verbs and adjectives.

Frodo Baggins is a character originally from a trilogy call [*called*] The Lord of the Rings, by J.R.R [*J.R.*] J. R. Tolkein. The book has now been make [*made*] into a film and the story is became [*is*] even famouser [*famous*] than it use to be. Frodo is not a human but a type of person called a

hobbit. Hobbits are more smaller than people but there is much about them that

is the same. Frodo is a hobbit who go [*went*] on a long and dangerous journey with other

hobbits and characters from the book. They has [*have*] to take a magical ring to the one

place where it could be destroy [*destroyed*] — the ring is very powerful and controls men in a

dark and mysterious way. By destroy [*destroying*] the ring, Frodo saved many people and

characters from the evil of the ring and the powers of the dark.

2 Now answer the following grammar questions about the text.

a) Find an example of a verb in the present simple. _____

b) Find an example of a comparative form. _____

c) Find an example of a verb in the past simple. _____

d) Find an example of the use of the passive. _____

e) Find an example of an expression which is also used to talk about the past. _____

f) Find the singular form of the noun 'people'. _____

g) Why do we say 'magical ring' and not 'magic ring'? _____

h) What is the singular form for the word 'men'? _____

3 Complete the following sentences by choosing the correct noun and verb from the boxes. The form of the verb will need to be changed.

> **Nouns**
> ~~horse~~ ~~homework~~ vet ~~school~~ ~~bike~~ authorities ~~holidays~~ ~~desks~~ ~~radio~~ ~~CD~~ hare ~~hand~~ ~~teacher~~ ~~bus~~ ~~letter~~ ~~film~~ ~~ice~~ ~~gum~~ ~~tap~~ ~~mobile phone~~

> **Verbs**
> ~~listen~~ ~~do~~ ~~raise~~ ~~write~~ ~~play~~ ~~sleep~~ ~~check~~ ~~borrow~~ ~~chew~~ ~~cycle~~ ~~grow~~ ~~ride~~ scribble ~~run~~ ~~freeze~~ ~~respect~~ ~~study~~ run ~~cry~~ ~~drink~~

a) I _listened_ to the concert on the _CD_ because I couldn't go to the theatre.

b) Don't _drink_ the water from the _tap_ – it doesn't taste very nice.

c) I have my own _radio_ and I _cycle_ it every day after school.

d) I _checked_ a _letter_ yesterday, which is amazing because normally I send emails.

e) She always _cries_ when she sees that _film_ because it is a very sad story.

f) The _ice_ is not _frozen_ yet because I just put it in the fridge.

g) The _horse_ _ran_ into the forest when it saw the man with his gun.

h) The boy _rode_ to school on his new _bike_ because he wanted to show it to his friends.

i) The children _ran_ for the _bus_ but they missed it by a second.

j) They _studied_ until 12 o' clock each day now they were on their _holidays_

k) They have a lot of _writing_ to do even if they are not at _school_ now.

l) She wants to be a _vet_ when she _grows_ up because she loves animals.

m) They asked if they could _borrow_ your new _radio_ but I said they would have to ask you.

n) The restaurant was recently _scribbled_ by the government _authorities_ because of a health scare.

o) The teacher asks that you __raise__ your __hand__ when you want to speak in class.

p) If the headmaster catches you __chewing__ __gum__ in the school, he will be very angry.

q) There is a bit of a problem at the school of children __sleeping__ on the school __desks__.

r) Your parents have to sign a book whenever you __divide__ the __homework__ that the teacher has set.

s) The children __respect__ their new __teacher__ because she has always been very fair with them.

t) If the teacher sees you __playing__ with your __mobile phone__ in the class, she will take it from you for a week!

4 Say whether the words below and on page 6 are nouns or verbs or if they can be both.
Then write a sentence using the one or both forms.

	Noun	Verb	Both
snow			✓

The snow lay on the ground. (noun)
It snowed all day. (verb)

	Noun	Verb	Both

a) respect ✓
She lost all respet from others.(noun)
Respet your family! (verb)

b) winter ✓
Winter is the coldest season of the year (noun)
I wintered on my grandfather's house (verb)

c) decide ✓
He decided to help anyone in need (verb)

d) put ✓

	Noun	Verb	Both
e) enjoy		✓	
f) connect		✓	
g) admire		✓	
h) anger			✓
i) improve		✓	
j) fly			✓

Skills

1 You are going to write an essay describing **one** of the pictures below. Use the guidelines for writing and effective planning in Unit 1 of your Coursebook (on pages 9 and 10) to help you. Write about 200 words.

2 Read the poem and complete the exercises below and on page 8.

> ### From The Pied Piper of Hamelin
>
> *Into the street the Piper stept,*
> *Smiling first a little smile,*
> *As if he knew what magic slept*
> *In his quiet pipe the while;*
> *Then, like a musical adept,*
> *To blow the pipe his lips he wrinkled,*
> *And green and blue his sharp eyes wrinkled*
> *Like a candle-flame where salt is sprinkled;*
> *And ere three shrill notes the pipe uttered,*
> *You heard if an army muttered;*
> *And the muttering grew to a grumbling;*
> *And the grumbling grew to a mighty rumbling;*
> *And out of the house the rats came tumbling.*
> *Great rats, small rats, lean rats, brawny rats,*
> *Brown rats, black rats, grey rats, tawny rats,*
> *Grave old plodders, gay young friskers*
> *Fathers, mothers, uncles, cousins,*
> *Cocking tails and pricking whiskers,*
> *Families by tens and dozens,*
> *Brothers, sisters, husbands, wives –*
> *Followed the Piper for their lives.*
> *From street to street he piped advancing,*
> *And step for step they followed dancing,*
> *Until they came to the river Weser*
> *Wherein all plunged and perished!*
>
> Robert Browning

a) Put the following pictures in the order they happen in the poem.

i)

5

ii)

3

iii)

8

iv)

1

v)

2

vi)

7

vii)

4

viii)

6

b) What words in the poem rhyme with the following?

    i) stept _adept_

    ii) smile _while_

    iii) wrinkled _sprinkled_

    iv) uttered _muttered_

    v) grumbling _rumbling_

    vi) friskers _whiskers_

    vii) cousins _dozens_

    viii) wives _lives_

    ix) advancing _dancing_

c) What **eight** family relationships are mentioned in the poem?

    Fathers   _Mothers_   _uncles_   _cousins_

    Brothers   _sisters_   _husbands_   _wives_

d) What **ten** types of rats are mentioned in the poem?

    Great rats   _small rats_   _lean rats_   _brawny rats_

    Brown r   _black r_   _grey r_   _tawny r_

Unit 2 Myths

Vocabulary

1 Match the words to their meanings.

1	imaginary	based on a myth	2
2	mythical	group of similar animals or plants	7
3	cryptozoology	loud or clear enough to be heard	4
4	audible	mythical one-horned horse	8
5	hibernate	not real, in the mind	1
6	consistently	piece of material with design	10
7	species	reliably, keeping the same standard	6
8	unicorn	set of clothes for particular job or school	9
9	uniform	the study of imaginary creatures	3
10	tapestry	sleep during winter months	5

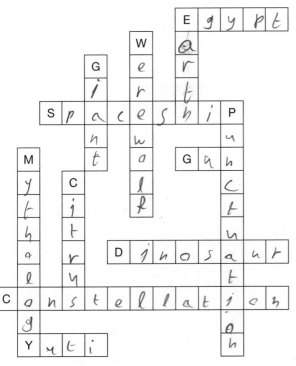

2 Do the following crossword.

- a group of stars forming a recognisable pattern
- based on old stories or events
- very large imaginary person
- person who becomes like a dog when the moon is full
- large creature like an ape, found in the mountains
- ancient animal which lived thousands of years ago
- the planet we live on
- word used to describe commas, full stops, hyphens, etc.
- used to describe fruit like lemons, oranges, grapefruit, etc.
- country where the River Nile is
- a hand weapon used by cowboys
- a vehicle for travelling in space

3 The letters of each word have been mixed up. Put them in their
correct order and write the word next to its meaning.

a) n a t m u u   _autumn_   before winter

b) d b i r u e   _buried_   to be covered under the ground

c) e a d i e n u c   _audience_   people who watch a show

d) h b e t a n e   _beneath_   under

e) b a l i u d e   _audible_   loud enough to hear

f) n n g n b i e i g   _beginning_   the start

g) l i e e e v b   _believe_   to think something is true

h) l b u e i a t f u   _beautiful_   lovely

4 Using the transcript from Unit 2, look at the picture and match the
words to the areas that are indicated.

~~door~~   eyes   ~~atmosphere~~   ~~moon 1~~   ~~moon 2~~   ~~surface~~
~~creature~~   scream   ~~mountains~~   peak   ~~teeth~~

5 Now match the words/expressions below to each of the words in Exercise 4 and write a complete sentence using both words. Put the sentences into the order they happened in the story. For example:

> The astronauts looked at each other with <u>nervous eyes</u>.

> ~~nervous~~ towering   with a hiss   gentle pink   huge, threatening and grey
> smaller, gentle glowing light   lush hair-like blue grass   piercing
> bird-like dinosaurs   razor-like   darker in colour

Grammar

1 Match the questions to the answers. For example:

> Who will be there? Anna.

What's your favourite lesson?

No, there isn't.

Maths.

Whose home is furthest from the school?

Very well, because I got the highest mark in the class.

Not until the summer.

With flour, eggs, milk and butter.

Where was football invented?

Which is the smallest of the planets?

Where were you born?

You enjoy drinking milk, don't you?

No, I prefer spring.

Yes, I do.

Yes, they can.

Yes, I can.

At home.

Do you enjoy going to school every day?

I don't know but maybe next week.

Do you think everybody should learn English?

How well did you do in your last test?

You like winter more than summer, don't you?

Yes, I do.

Paris.

Mercury.

When are you next going to the cinema?

You would like to visit Disneyland, wouldn't you?

England.

Michael's because it takes an hour to get here.

Who's climbed a mountain?

Can you dance well?

When is the next school holiday?

There is a swimming pool near your school, isn't there?

Yes, I do.

What is the capital of France?

Which country is famous for its spaghetti?

Yes, I would love to.

How are cakes made?

Italy

Can cats swim?

I have.

2 Choose the correct word for each sentence.

> The girl left ~~she~~/her/~~herself~~ bag.

a) Have they ever been/went/go to the seaside?

b) The cat walked under/along/above the wall.

c) The train leaves on/in/at 12.00.

d) That bag belongs to his/him/he.

e) Mark and Joe are nice boys but Mark and Joe/he/they are noisy.

f) The plane leaves on/at/in the 21st of April not the 24th!

g) He/It/Him bought a new camera because the old one was broken.

h) The dog is lying beneath/on/at the tree.

i) They seen/see/saw a great film the other day.

j) They praised him because he/his/him did well in he/his/him test.

k) The man walked into/through/in the door and bumped his head.

l) We should be finished at/in/on an hour so please wait.

m) They eat/eaten/ate snails and didn't like them.

n) Her/She/Herself diary was read by someone and her/she/herself is not very happy.

o) A/An/The river has flooded again because of the rain.

p) A/The/An sheep have escaped into the road again.

3 In these sentences the verbs are in the present. Rewrite each sentence, changing the verbs into the past. You may need to change the sentence slightly for the meaning. For example:

> Our baby <u>cries</u> and then <u>screams</u> for food.
> Yesterday our baby cried and screamed for food.

a) He <u>breaks</u> many glasses when he <u>begins</u> to put them away.
   Yesterday he broke many glasses when he began to put them aw

b) Every time the wind <u>blows</u> the plants <u>fall</u> off the wall. When the wind ___blew___ yesterday the plants fell off the wall.

c) Mark always <u>builds</u> a sandcastle when he goes to the beach.
   Last week Mark built a sandcastle when he went to the be

d) She <u>buys</u> a souvenir whenever she <u>visits</u> a different country.
   She ___bought a souvenir when she visited___ Italy.

e) They <u>sit</u> in the garden every evening and <u>drink</u> tea.
   They sat in the garden every evening and drank tea

4 Now change the following sentences from the past to the present.

a) The dry wood <u>burst</u> into flames and the fire <u>spread</u> quickly.

The dry wood *bursts into fames and the fire spreads quickly*

b) He ate a whole chocolate cake yesterday when he visited grandma.

He *eats a whole chocolate cke whenever he visits grandma*

c) They bought a new car last year and sold it again yesterday.

They *buy a new car today and will sell it again*

d) They <u>slept</u> until very late this morning because they <u>went</u> to bed late last night.

They *sleep very late at morning because they go to bed late*

e) The children always <u>fought</u> over small things and <u>argued</u> a lot.

The children always *fight over small things and argue a lot*

Skills

1 For each of the statements below and on page 14, write **one** comment against the statement and **one** in favour.

a) School uniforms should be worn at school.

In favour: *That's because they make students equal*

Against: *students need to express themselves throug their cloths*

b) Young people should not be allowed to buy cigarettes.

In favour: *Cigarettes are really unhealthy to old people but even more dangerous ta yong people*

Against: *Young people have the rights to buy what they want.*

c) Mobile phones should not be allowed at school.

In favour: *Students wont's be able to put their focus on the lessons.*

Against: *Mobil phones have a very important prt in every one's life*

d) Young adults of 16 should be allowed to drive cars.

In favour: _It makes it easier for young adult to move from place to place to get their needs._

Against: _Yeng people are not capeble enough to drive well as adult people_

e) Young adults should be allowed to vote at 16.

In favour: _Every one has the right to vote including young adults_

Against: _Not all young adults are wise enough to vote_

f) Schools should not give homework every day.

In favour: _Students need more free time to play_

Against: _Students need homework every day to strength_

2 Now look at some comments made about the subjects below. Rewrite them so that they are more objective and formal.

> It is so stupid because when we have a test at school we are not allowed to use our computers. I've told the teachers how silly this is because we use our computers all the time and 'write' much more quickly on them than we do with a pen and pencil. The teachers think we are going to cheat because they do not understand that we do things differently from them.

> Teachers should be allowed to smoke in the school if they want to. I mean, does the school think that we don't know which of our teachers smoke and which don't? There is so much advertising around nowadays about smoking that if some kid thinks it is clever to smoke then who's the stupid one? We don't need schools to hide things like that from us.

3 Read the following extract and do the exercises that follow.

The story of the pan pipes

Zeus, the king of the Greek gods, argued frequently with his wife, Hera. Many of these arguments were about young women, of whom Zeus was particularly fond. Unfortunately, it was often these young women who came off the worst from the arguments. Take the case of Io, for example. No sooner had Zeus fallen in love with her than he was forced to change her into a white heifer (a young cow) to keep her out of Hera's sight. But then Hera discovered the trick, captured Io and locked her up in a gloomy cave where she was guarded by a monster called Argus. Argus was well suited to the task because he had no less than one hundred eyes. No matter how long or how heavily he slept, at least two of these eyes would always remain open – so poor Io could never escape.

a) In Unit 1 of this Workbook you read about the Pied Piper and his pipes. What did the pipes do to the rats? *It attracted the rats.*

b) How do you think the pan pipes will be used in this story? Write an ending to this story of about 200 words explaining how the pan pipes were used.

c) Draw a picture to illustrate the story. Follow these instructions:

- Draw Argus in the centre of the box.
- Draw Io in the cave with Argus watching her.
- Draw Zeus looking down from Mount Olympus (in Greece) surrounded by clouds.
- Draw Hera wearing a long white dress. She is looking angrily at Zeus.
- In your picture include how you used the pan pipes in the story.

Unit 3 World mysteries

Vocabulary

1 Find **13** words in the wordsearch and write them in the box below. All the words can be found in Unit 3 of the Coursebook.

```
N R C O N Q U I S T A D O R S K
I S O L A T E D F L J R V X T V
H Z K L G C O U N T R Y S I D E
P R E H I S T O R I C K F G N H
V A C T J M M Q B W N F C H D I
N S B K M N O D B U T I Z N I C
M P T Z T P L N S K F T Z R S L
B H A W Y O V P U I R Q X P A E
V Y P T G N P L C M R M V X P S
N X R R L H C A L R E O R Q X B
Y I F L V A P T Q K N N L C E N
H A I F N F N O J A K T T J A T
N T F T M N M T C V Y M L S R F
Y I K J A M L L I N C W K N E Q
X O X N H L O X X C X N W J D X
M N Y N M V Y E X P L O R E R S
```

1. Atlantic 2. explorers 3. Pacific. 4. monument
5. isolated. 6. prehistoric 7. countryside 8. gold
9. asphyxiation 10. volcano 11. Italy 12. plato
13. sunk 14. conquistadors

2 Now match the words from the wordsearch to the following definitions.

- the largest of the oceans between Asia, Australia and America _pacific ocean_
- to be alone and very separate _isolated_
- the ocean between the continents of America, Europe and Africa _Atlantic ocean_
- a very famous ancient Greek Philosopher _Plato_
- to go under because it is heavier than water _sunk_
- from the period before history was written _prehistoric_
- area of land where not many people live, but there are farms, trees, etc. _countryside_

- an object built to remember somebody, an event or action _monument_
- a burning mountain _Volcano_
- a place in Europe that has a shape like a boot _Italy_
- prevented from breathing _asphyxiation_
- a very valuable metal _gold_
- early Spanish travellers _conquistadars_
- people who are the first to go and find places and objects _explorers_

3 The letters of each word have been mixed up. Put them in their correct order and write the word next to its meaning.

a) m b i l c _climb_ you do this up a mountain

b) n c c s o l n i u o _conclusion_ the end

c) l c c o t e h a o _chocalate_ made from the cocoa bean

d) s s s b n e i u _buisness_ trade/work, etc.

e) m o l c u n _column_ a narrow piece of writing

f) c c t t o o n n n e r a i _concentration_ look at something very carefully

g) g a c h t u _caught_ held safely in the hand

Grammar

1 Match each of the words on the left with its use on the right.

a ever	in questions and negations a
b never	to talk about something that was done/happened a minute ago c
c just	to express a starting point f
d yet	in questions d
e already	to express a period of time g
f since	to talk about something not done at all b
g for	to talk about before the time in question e

2 Now use each of the words to complete the sentences below.

a) I haven't seen that film _for_ ages.

b) Haven't you finished that book _yet_?

c) Will you _ever_ listen to what you're being told?

d) The film has _just_ started if you were planning to watch it.

e) They _never_ even try to read a book, it is always computers.

f) How long is it _since_ you started doing ballet?

g) They have _already_ left because they couldn't wait any longer.

3 Look at the following drawings – match each one with its sentence on page 19.

A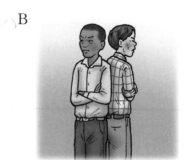

B

C

D

E

F

G

H

I

J

a) It has just started snowing so we had better not go out now.
Picture ___C___

b) She has been working there for 15 years now and wants to leave.
Picture ___G___

c) Have you ever done bungee jumping? Picture ___J___

d) They haven't talked to each other since last year. Picture
___B___

e) She is still knitting that jumper and hasn't finished it yet.
Picture ___A___

f) They have never eaten snails before. Picture ___E___

g) He has already gone to bed. Picture ___F___

h) She has already cooked the dinner. Picture ___I___

i) They have been studying now for two hours. Picture ___H___

j) The phone just rang as I walked out the front door.
Picture ___D___

4 Follow the instructions and draw the picture depending on your answer.

- Have you ever walked to school?
  If 'yes' draw a square head. If 'no' draw a round head.
- Have you ever been abroad?
  If 'yes' draw a happy face. If 'no' draw a sad face.
- Have you ever failed any exams?
  If 'yes' draw a thick neck. If 'no' draw a thin neck.
- Have you ever been on a ferry boat?
  If 'yes' draw short hair on your person. If 'no' draw long hair.
- Have you ever had a tooth taken out at the dentist?
  If 'yes' draw big ears on your person. If 'no' draw small ears.
- Have you ever stayed overnight in a hospital?
  If 'yes' draw a fat body. If 'no' draw a thin body.
- Have you ever had a pet hamster or cat?
  If 'yes' draw long arms. If 'no' draw short arms.
- Have you ever stayed up all night?
  If 'yes' draw skinny legs. If 'no' draw fat legs.
- Have you ever cheated in a test?
  If 'yes' draw big feet. If 'no' draw small feet.
- Have you ever had swimming lessons?
  If 'yes' draw long fingers. If 'no' draw short fingers.
- Have you ever lied to your parents?
  If 'yes' draw a hamster next to your person. If 'no' draw a cat.
- Have you ever tried Japanese food?
  If 'yes' draw a bowl of food next to your animal. If 'no' draw a bowl
  of water.

5 Complete the following sentences about yourself in an interesting way.

- I have tried to _cock in the kitchen but the result!_
- I have met _my best friend whom I haven't seen in years_
- I have seen _wonderful scenes in different countries._
- I have bought _a modern car but I need to learn more about its technolo_
- I have travelled to _China but I was surprised by their food!_
- I have never _been to Atlantis as I couldn't find it_
- I have lost _my dog a year ago but I found him again with five puppies!_
- I have broken _my mom's vase while I was trying flowers in it_
- I have nearly _finished drawing a portrait of myself_
- I have listened to _my music collections so I had to change my headphones three times._

Skills

1 Read the text on page 22 and say what the following pictures show.

a)

b)

c)

_____

d)

_____

e)

_____

f)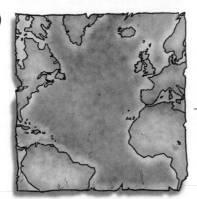

_____

g)

h)

The Mary Celeste departed from New York with its new captain, Captain Briggs, in 1872. With him were his wife and young daughter, and eight crew members. The ship was bound for Genoa, Italy, with a full cargo. The captain, his family and the crew were never seen again and it is unlikely that the events leading to their disappearance will ever be known with certainty. The Mary Celeste was later discovered drifting but with nobody on board – lack of evidence ruled out piracy or foul play. The ship was called a 'ghost ship' because although it was in a mess, it was also completely empty and all of the ship's papers, apart from the captain's logbook, were missing. The logbook was dated 24 November 1872. Aboard the ship was enough food and water to last for six months. Also, it was strange that the life boat appeared to have been intentionally launched, suggesting that the ship had been deliberately abandoned.

2 Find words in the text which mean the following:

a) left _departed_

b) group or team _crew_

c) travelling to _bound_

d) floating with no aim _drifting_

e) criminal actions _piracy_

f) diary _logbook_

g) deliberately _intentionally_

h) released _launched._

i) proof _evidence_

3 What do you think happened to the *Mary Celeste*?

Imagine that you were on the *Mary Celeste* and lived to say what happened. Choose which of the characters you wish to be and tell your story from their point of view. Include as many details as you can about the events which led to the disappearance of all the people on board the ship.

Vocabulary

1 Use the definitions below to make words to complete the word snake.

- This is a large instrument. It's usual colours are black and white. *piano*
- These were made from empty barrels. *drums*
- You hit these and they make a powerful beat. *steel pans*
- We saw this instrument in Unit 2 of this Workbook. *pan pipes*
- The Chinese do this as part of their musical theatre. *acrobatics*
- These instruments use air to produce sound. *suling*
- The harp and violin are examples of this type of instrument. *orchestral*
- This kind of music is made not with instruments but by using one machine. *electronic*
- Many different instruments are used to produce this kind of music. *wind*
- This music represents a culture. *ethnic*
- These are used to produce music. There are many different types. *instruments*
- This consists of very dramatic singing and music. You see it at the theatre. *opera*

2 Now use the words from the snake to complete the following sentences.

a) They are a great band but none of them knows how to play a traditional instrument so all their music is *electronic*

b) Because they weren't allowed any musical instruments they made their own by using old *steel pans*

c) *Drums* music can be produced by as many as 100 people or as few as ten.

d) In any one country there can be many types of _ethnic_ music, because each group of people has its own type.

e) The trumpet is a big _swing_ instrument and can make very powerful sounds.

f) Most _instruments_ can be quite difficult to learn and it takes time and patience.

g) The _acrobatics_ done by the young girls were truly amazing. Their bodies were like rubber!

h) The violin is a beautiful _orchestral_ instrument which can produce wonderful sounds.

i) _Wind_ used to be used to send messages, before the time of the telephone.

j) The Pied Piper's _pan pipes_ produce a sound that only rats can hear.

k) We are going to see the _opera_ Madame Butterfly – I've never been to one before, so I hope I like it.

l) The _piano_ is a very expensive instrument and not easy to carry around.

3 The letters of each word have been mixed up. Put the letters into the correct order and write the word next to its meaning.

a) g d u t r e a h   _daughter_ female child
b) d f n t e i i e   _definite_ 100%
c) t n u s c i o o n u _continuous_ keeps on going
d) q c s o c e e e n u n _consequence_ the result
e) t c o n e i r a   _reaction_ response to something
f) s d g n i e   _design_ a drawing or plan
g) u s o o s i n c c   _conscious_ knowing what is happening
h) s o c d e i i n   _decision_ choice

4 Look at the table below and on page 26. Find the words in the left column in your dictionary and complete the table.

Word	Section	Page	Head word of page	Word before/after	Meaning
conscientious					
	Example sentence:				

Word	Section	Page	Head word of page	Word before/after	Meaning
miniscule					
Example sentence:					
topiary					
Example sentence:					
suffragette					
Example sentence:					

Grammar

1 Write all the letters of the alphabet

1	2	3	4	5	6	7	8	9	10	11	12	13
a	b	c	d	e	f	g	h	i	j	k	l	m

14	15	16	17	18	19	20	21	22	23	24	25	26
n	o	p	q	r	s	t	u	v	w	x	y	z

Now work out what these nouns are, using the code.

a) 1 13 2 9 20 9 15 14   ambition
b) 12 9 20 20 5 18   litter
c) 2 15 20 20 12 5   bottle
d) 4 9 19 3 9 16 12 9 14 5   discipline
e) 3 15 13 16 21 20 5 18   computer
f) 16 1 19 19 9 15 14   passion
g) 4 9 3 20 9 15 14 1 18 25   dictionary
h) 18 5 7 18 5 20   regret
i) 9 14 6 15 18 13 1 20 9 15 14   information

2   Decide whether the nouns in Exercise 1 are abstract, concrete or
    collective. Write them in the correct columns.

Abstract	Concrete	Collective
ambition	litter	dictionary
discipline	bottle	information
passion	computer	
regret		

3   Match the nouns to the following definitions.

   a) Something we have at school to keep us in place. _discipline_

   b) Something we feel when we haven't done something we think we
      should. _regret_

   c) We use this to find the meanings of words. _dictionary_

   d) Things we throw away. _litter_

   e) We use this for many things, including games, typing, research, etc.
      computer

   f) When you are not happy with what you have got, and want more.
      ambition

   g) Details about something. _information_

   h) Used for putting liquid in. _bottle_

   i) A word which is stronger than love. _passion_

4   Look at the following picture. Think of different nouns that you could
    use to describe it. Think of at least **four** nouns for each category on
    page 28.

horse, aggressive, army. Land

Abstract	Concrete	Collective
a gressive	land	army
angry	horse	stable
tenseness	solidare	brigade
brave	weapons	cache

5 Pair up the words and phrases to make **12** collective nouns. For example:

> a gaggle of geese

fish grapes a choir of people wolves theatre goers a pack of
caterpillars cows a crowd of a band of an army of birds
a school of directors a board of singers a colony of a bunch of
robbers a herd of an audience of a flock of penguins

6 Complete the following sentences using the collective nouns from Exercise 5.

a) The ___board of directors___ have called a meeting at 12.00 o'clock.

b) The last ___bunch of grapes___ was hanging from the vine.

c) At Christmas a ___choir of singers___ always visits the old people's home and sings traditional songs.

d) A ___crowd of people___ rushed to the bus to get on but it was full.

e) A ___herd of cows___ were taken to a different field where the grass was greener.

f) A ___flock of birds___ flew over the field and made a beautiful sight.

g) A ___band of robbers___ were caught by the police as they were leaving the shop.

h) A ___pack of wolves___ attacked the sheep and frightened them all away.

i) The ___colony of penguins___ found the ice they were living on getting smaller and smaller.

j) A ___school of fish___ were seen up the river near the fishing grounds.

k) An _army of caterpillars_ ate all the green leaves on the new plants.

l) The _audience of theatre goers_ got angry because the play started late.

Skills

1 Read the following text and answer the questions on page 30.

The story is from a book called *The Ring O' Bells Mystery*, in which some children visit an old house, and are shown around by an old woman.

The children followed the old woman round the mansion. It felt a dead, forgotten place, and everywhere struck cold, that lovely May morning. Diana shivered. She didn't like any of it much.

The woman recited long strings of facts about the old place, but she didn't make them sound very interesting.

'In 1645 Hugh Dourley lived in this Hall, and it was he who first caused it to be called Ring O' Bells,' she droned on.

'Why?' asked Snubby, his interest caught at last.

'He had a peal of bells put in the south tower,' said the woman, beginning to gabble. 'He rang them when he had anything to rejoice about. But one night they rang themselves, so it's said – and it wasn't because there was anything to rejoice about, either. His eldest son had been killed, and he didn't know. But the bells rang at the very moment of his death.'

This sounded rather weird. The children were now at the bottom of the square south tower. A small spiral stairway went up, and they wondered if they might climb it.

'Yes, climb up if you want to,' said the woman. 'You'll see the bells hanging there, high up. They say they're still the same ones that Hugh Dourley put in, but it stands to reason they can't be.'

The children climbed up the stairway. It was steep and narrow and twisted sharply, so that it was difficult to climb without slipping.

At the top of the stairway was a small platform. The children looked up, and saw, high above their heads, a cluster of bells, hanging silently on what looked like thick ropes.

Snubby stared at the bells, and his hands itched to ring them. Snubby always liked anything that made a loud noise.

'Can we ring them?' he asked, feeling, of course, perfectly certain of the answer.

a) Find **three** words that suggest the mansion is not a 'friendly' place.
dead, forgotten, and cold.

b) How can we tell that the woman is not interested in telling the children about the mansion? *because the women recited long string of facts about the old place, but she didn't make the sound interesting.*

c) How do the children get up to see the bells? *through climbing the stairway*

d) Why does it 'stand to reason' that the bells are not the same ones?

e) The bells normally rang when there was something to rejoice about. What happened one night that was different? *The bells rang themselves, and there was nothing to rejoice about either.*

f) Snubby likes things that make loud noises, like bells. Name **two** other musical instruments that make loud noises. *Octobass steel pans*

g) In line 6 we see the word 'Hall'. Why is a capital letter used? *because it is a name*

h) Find words in the text which mean the same as the following:

   i) to talk in a boring way *drone*

   ii) strange *weird*

   iii) round and round *spiral*

   iv) felt *feeling*

i) Find a collective term *'strings' of fact*

j) In your own words, explain how you feel about the following part of the story:

> But one night they rang themselves, so it's said – and it wasn't because there was anything to rejoice about, either. His eldest son had been killed, and he didn't know. But the bells rang at the very moment of his death. *It felt a little creepy and strange but I believe the son's soul rang the bells.*

2 What do you think happens next? Write about 200 words and explain how you think the story ends.

3 Ask somebody to dictate the first **13** lines of the text to you (up to '… at the very moment of his death'). As you write, remember to include all the necessary punctuation. Time yourself as you write, then write it again and see whether you are quicker the second time.

Unit 5 | Modern music

Vocabulary

1 Find the **20** words in the word snake.

2 Write the words in alphabetical order.

3 Now match each of the words to its meaning.

   a) sweet and dry and you eat them   *biscuit*

   b) it is red and you put it on your potato chips   *ketchup*

   c) the production of sounds electronically   *synthesist*

   d) a flat meal made with eggs and fried   *omelette*

   e) a large ape-like animal   *gorilla*

   f) where young children go to learn and play   *kindergarten*

   g) material used to make popular blue trousers   *denim*

   h) we need it to see at night   *light*

   i) we put it round our neck to keep warm   *scarf*

   j) we need to use this small room every day   *lavatory*

   k) people from the south west of Europe   *Bengali*

   l) group of people, all the same age   *generation*

  m) an Asian language   *Spanish*

   n) music that not many people like   *punk*

   o) not being fair and equal   *discrimination*

   p) the words of a song   *lyrics*

   q) a problem   *dilemma*

   r) music that most people like   *pop*

   s) music from the Caribbean   *???*

   t) a band that had lots of its music played in the film *Mamma Mia*   *abba*

4 Complete the dialogue below using the words from the box. You will need to change the form of the words as you use them.

announce suggest order grumble boast insist add promise threat question explain venture

'You've never let me learn an instrument,' _ventured_ Maria to her mother.

'You've never asked,' _grumbled_ her mother, and _added_ 'I couldn't afford the lessons anyway.'

'You could let me go and get a job so I can get the money,' _suggested_ Maria.

'How can you go out and earn money?' _questioned_ her mother.

'I'm 16 now,' _boasted_ Maria.

'Yes, but you have never worked before,' _explained_ her mother.

'Well if you don't let me go and look for work, I'm going to anyway!' _threatened_ Maria.

'Don't speak to me like that!' _ordered_ her mother.

'I want to learn to play an instrument,' _insisted_ Maria.

'Well, actually, I have booked guitar lessons for your birthday,' _announced_ her mother.

'Mum, thank you! I'll become the best guitarist ever!' _promised_ Maria.

5 The letters of each word have been mixed up. Put them in their correct order and write the word next to its meaning.

a) y e g r n e   _energy_   power or force

b) y d r a i   _diary_   a place to write daily events

c) s s b a a e r m r   _embarrass_ to make shy or uncomfortable

d) n e g e e t a n m g   _agreement_ a fixed arrangement

e) d d m n i a o   _diamond_   a beautiful stone

f) p p d s n t o i a i   _disappoint_ let down or upset

g) p p a a i e d s r   _disappear_   vanish or go away

h) t l p d m v e e e o n   _development_ growth or training

Grammar

1 Rewrite the passage below in the style of a dialogue, adding the punctuation listed.

> capital letters   commas   full stops   speech marks   question marks
> exclamation marks   apostrophes

have you finished your homework yet asked his father no not yet answered aresti because im finding it very difficult is there anything I can do to help offered his father it would be great if you could but its algebra and its not easy said aresti algebra was my strongest subject at school boasted his father yeah well lets see how much you can remember then said aresti umm pondered his father maybe it has changed since I was a kid well let me show you some things then ventured aresti it might help you remember yes that would be a good idea said his father but let me get my glasses first

2 Look at the following pictures and write a dialogue for each one. In your dialogue, explain the situation so that the reader knows what has happened and what the people are talking about. Make sure that you use punctuation correctly.

a)

b)

c)

d)

3 Change the following sentences from indirect to direct speech.

a) Michael was told to be quiet and to sit down.
"Sit down and be quiet, Michael."

b) The air steward asked the passengers if they would turn off their mobile phones. *"Could you turn off your mobile phones?"*

c) The shop assistant asked the customer if they had any change. *"Do you have any change?"*

d) The girl asked the boy if she could borrow his pencil. *"Can I borrow your pencil?"*

e) The loud speaker told everybody to check in at desk four. *"Everybody check in at desk four."*

f) The policeman asked the man if he had seen anybody walking around with a stolen bag. *"Have you seen anybody walking around with a stolen bag?"*

g) The man asked how he could use the Excel program on his computer. *"How could I use the Excel program on my computer?"*

h) The librarian told him to bring back the books he had taken out of the library. *"You have to bring back the books you have taken out of the library."*

i) The lieutenant ordered the soldiers to run up the hill. *"Run up to the hill, soldiers!"*

j) The vet asked if the cat had eaten that day. *"Has the cat eaten today?"*

Skills

1 Read the text on pages 34 to 36 and find the following information.

a) Who is also an actress? *Madonna*

b) Which singer is connected to the law? *Sting*

c) Whose father is a famous singer too? *Enrique Iglesias*

d) Which **two** bands had members who had unhappy ends? *The Beatles, Queen*

e) Which singer didn't want to live in the real world? *Michael Jackson*

f) Who plays string instruments? *Amy MacDonald*

g) Who connects a princess and a rose? *Elton John*

h) Who has many men in her life? *Victoria Beckham*

i) Which Scandanavian band travels abroad? *Nightwish*

j) Who sang about a tragic story? *Celine Dion*

k) Which band's songs are in a popular film? *abba*

Abba
- They won a Eurovision song contest.
- The band is made up of two men and two women.
- Their songs are in the film Mamma Mia.

The Beatles

- They were from Liverpool in England.
- John Lennon was murdered in New York.
- They were fashion icons in their time.

Celine Dion

- She is French Canadian.
- She sang the theme tune for the film Titanic.
- She came to fame in a song show.

Elton John

- His real name is Reg Dwight.
- He plays the piano.
- He wrote the song Goodbye England's Rose for Princess Diana's funeral.

Amy MacDonald

- She is a country and western singer.
- She is Scottish.
- Her main instruments are the guitar and piano.

Enrique Iglesias

- He is the son of Julio – another famous singer.
- He sings duets with other famous singers.
- He is from Spain.

Madonna

- She sang with Justin Timberlake.
- She adopted two children from Africa.
- She played the role of Evita in the film.

Nightwish
- They are a Finnish band.
- They were inspired by the composer Hans Zimmer.
- They play concerts internationally.

Michael Jackson
- His home in America was called 'Neverland'.
- He was one of the Jackson Five.
- He died at the age of 50.

Queen
- Their lead singer Freddie Mercury died of AIDS.
- Their song Bohemian Rhapsody was the first song made into a visual track.
- A symphony has been written based on their songs.

Victoria Beckham
- She was a member of the band The Spice Girls.
- She is married to the famous footballer David Beckham.
- She has three sons.

Sting
- He used to sing with the band The Police.
- He sang a famous duet with the singer Mary J. Blige.
- He was a main singer at the charity show Live Aid.

2 Choose **one** of the following topics and write a narrative of about 200 words. Use the section on narrative writing in your Coursebook to help you.

- A holiday I'll never forget
- The day my friend came
- The day it happened

Vocabulary

1 In the box you will find **ten** objects and the sounds they can make. Match them up and then use them to complete the sentences below.

> aeroplane   ringing   meowing   bells   ticking   dog   clock
> shouting   baby   crying   doors   barking   droning   cat   glass
> banging   clanging   mobile phone   shattering   children

a) The _baby_ started _crying_ because he wanted something to eat.

b) The football went over the fence and the children heard the _glass_ of the greenhouse _shattering_

c) The sound of the _doors_ _banging_ over the houses was very annoying.

d) The _aeroplane_ kept _clanging_ because Barnaby hadn't closed them properly.

e) The _children_ were _shouting_ as they played their game of volleyball.

f) The _cat_ was _meowing_ because it wanted a dish of milk.

g) The _bells_ started _ringing_ as the bride and groom walked out of the church.

h) The _clock_ was _ticking_ the minutes away as the test got near the end.

i) The _dog_ started _barking_ as the man went near the gate of its house.

j) _Mobile phones droning_ are not allowed in the classroom under any circumstances.

2 Fit the words below into the grid.

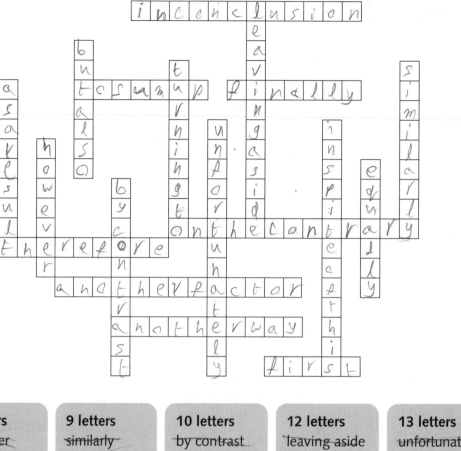

5 letters	7 letters	9 letters	10 letters	12 letters	13 letters
~~first~~	~~however~~	~~similarly~~	~~by contrast~~	~~leaving aside~~	~~unfortunately~~
	~~equally~~	~~therefore~~	~~another way~~	~~in conclusion~~	~~another~~
	~~finally~~	~~as a result~~			~~factor~~
	~~to sum up~~	~~turning to~~			~~on the~~
	~~but also~~				~~contrary~~
					~~in spite of~~
					~~this~~

3 Now put the words from Exercise 2 into the correct categories.

Contrast/ opposite	Similarity	Sequence/ addition	Consequence/ conclusion	Other
by contrast	equally	first	to sum up	turning to
another way	similarly	however	therefore	leaving aside
another factor		finally	as a result	
on the contrary		but also	in conclusion	
in spite of this			unfortunately	

4 Look at the pictures and write a sentence to describe each one. Use some of the words from Exercise 3.

a)

The mother and her son started making a cake using the first ingredient.

b)

The lecturer explained the similarity of teenage smokers between France and Italy.

c)

The student compared the obeity level in poor and rich countries, unfortunately the rich countries have a high level of obesity

d)

The teacher asked the students to stop claping, however some of them continued to clap.

e)

The teacher showed the entrast between the weather of a decert and the North pole

5 The letters of each word have been mixed up. Put them in their correct order and write the word next to its meaning.

a) y t o f r — *forty* — four decades
b) i e e e d v c n — *evidence* — proof
c) q u r e e n i — *require* — to ask
d) y r u f r e b a — *february* — the second month
e) t e e o n i v m n n r — *environment* — our surroundings
f) a a e i u t n v o l — *evaluation* — close inspection
g) e e r c f i — *fierce* — angry or dangerous
h) x p a a n n e l t o i — *explnation* — more detail

Grammar

1 A dialogue between a teacher and Sara and another between Michael and Emily have been mixed up. Sort them out.

e	Michael	Well, what about Sunday?
7	Michael	No, it's not okay. Bye. See you around.
6	Teacher	Okay then. But make sure you find out the lessons that you missed in class.
h	Emily	'Michael day' comes when I'm free. Okay?
c	Michael	How about Saturday night then?
d	Emily	That would be better, except I promised to take my sister shopping.
3	Sara	Well, my mother has made a dentist appointment for me.
7	Sara	Yes sir, thank you.
1	Sara	Excuse me sir, but I will need the day off school tomorrow.
a	Michael	Shall we go to the cinema tomorrow?
b	Emily	Can we make it another night? My grandparents are coming over for dinner.
g	Michael	But it has been family day every day! What about 'Michael day'?
4	Teacher	Could you not go in the afternoon when school has finished?
2	Teacher	Why's that then, Sara?
5	Sara	My mother tried to make an appointment but the dentist was full.
f	Emily	Sorry Michael, Sunday is family day and my parents won't let me come.

2 Now report the two dialogues. Look at Let's do some grammar in the Coursebook (page 69) to help you.

3 Look at the following pictures.

  i) Imagine what the people are saying and write the dialogue.

  ii) When you have written the dialogues, report the story and what was said. Imagine that you are writing the report for a newspaper. An example is given on page 42.

a)

i) Thief: Open the drawer and give me the money!

ii) Employee: Ok, ok, just don't shot.

b)

i) Bob: What have you done?! you crashed into my car!!

ii) Steve: No! It was your fault! You passed the red sign!!

c)

i) Seller: The is a new house. I am sure you will find it good.

ii) Wife: Yes it is beautiful, but it is too expesive.

d)

i) Teacher: Don't do trouble again! or I will punish you!

ii) Student: Sorry, we will never repeat this again.

For example:

> **a) i)** Bank robber: Hand over any cash you've got there.
> Cashier: _____
>
> **ii)** A robber went into a major bank earlier today. He went up to a cashier and told her to _____.

4 Answer the following questions about yourself.

a) What have you grumbled about recently?

b) What have you promised recently?

c) Has somebody ordered you to do something recently? What was it?

d) Has somebody threatened you over anything recently? What was it?

e) Have you or any of your friends boasted about anything recently? What was it?

f) Have you enquired about anything recently?

g) Did anybody have to emphasise anything to you recently? What was it?

h) Have you needed anything to be explained to you recently? What was it?

Skills

1 Read the following text and underline the **five** sounds that are mentioned.

Church bells <u>ring</u> the time, street sellers <u>cry</u> out their products, telling us what they have for sale today, singers push the latest <u>scandal</u>, and music comes from tavern doors: these are the sounds of London in the 17th century. Amongst the many noises, even the silence of the night is broken by the bellman's <u>ringing</u> and accompanying call, 'Past one of the clock, and a cold, frosty, windy morning.'

These are the sounds of early modern England that lead you through the streets into taverns and theatres, to dances, cathedral services and individual homes. It shows what life was like in the 17th century as they <u>echo</u> like ghosts through the city. The sad fact is that all that remains of these times and noises are books, images and musical instruments. The sounds themselves have long since vanished and only our imagination can take us back in time to hear the sounds that the people of that time heard.

2 Decide whether each of the following statements is true or false about 17th-century London.

a) People have watches to tell the time.

b) Singers are the same as modern-day newspapers or magazines.

c) The sounds are similar to those of modern-day London.

d) The bellman is like the radio.

e) You can still hear these sounds in London.

f) The atmosphere now exists only on paper.

g) We can only imagine what London of the 17th century was like.

h) The sounds mentioned are very different from those of modern-day London.

3 The text on page 42 uses quite colourful language to describe what London was like in the 17th century. Using the text above to help you, think of a:

a) simile

b) metaphor

c) personification

that you could use to further describe London in those days. For example:

> The church bell's toll was as cold as the night.

4 Write a paragraph of about 100 words describing the sounds where you live. Try to make your writing as interesting as possible.

Unit 7 Pictures

Vocabulary

1 Write all the letters of the alphabet

1	2	3	4	5	6	7	8	9	10	11	12	13
a	b	c	___	___	___	___	___	___	___	___	___	___

14	15	16	17	18	19	20	21	22	23	24	25	26
___	___	___	___	___	___	___	___	___	___	___	___	___

Now work out what these words are, using the code.

a) 19 1 3 18 5 4   _____

b) 16 18 5 8 9 19 20 15 18 9 3   _____

c) 19 20 5 5 16   _____

d) 5 14 7 18 1 22 5 4   _____

e) 16 5 18 9 15 4   _____

f) 19 1 14 3 20 21 1 18 25   _____

g) 20 18 21 19 20 25   _____

h) 3 21 12 20 21 18 5   _____

i) 19 20 21 13 2 12 5   _____

j) 19 9 20 5 19   _____

2 Match up these half-words to make a synonym for each of the words above. For example:

faithful

ho	ing
anc	ly
tr	~~ful~~
civili	tions
im	ter
shel	sation
slop	ip
~~faith~~	me
loca	printed
ti	ient

3 Look at the following groups of words. Use the words and phrases in the box to write **two** sentences about each group. One of the sentences should describe a similarity and the other should describe a difference. You can use the words and phrases more than once if you mish.

> like   unlike   on the other hand   but   in the same way   also
> nonetheless   however   likewise   rather than   in contrast with
> similarly   as both   instead

For example:

> lizard, butterfly, bird
> A butterfly can fly in the same way that a bird can.
> A lizard lives for a long time, unlike a butterfly.

a) beach, mountains, countryside

b) grammar, mathematics, physics

c) books, magazines, newspapers

d) adult, child, babies

e) Argentina, Brazil, Spain

f) milk, margarine, butter

g) olive trees, apple trees, lemon trees

h) cement, iron, paper

4 The letters of each word have been mixed up. Put them in their correct order and write the word next to its meaning.

a) g h t h e i   _____ how tall someone/something is

b) l l f f u i   _____ to complete

c) p m v s r o e i i   _____ get along or make do

d) m r t o u r h f r e e   _____ also

e) t l e h a h   _____ fitness

f) a a y g n m i i r   _____ not real

g) d h p a p e n e   _____ done or finished

h) d g a u r   _____ protect

Grammar

1 Put the sentences below into the correct box.

Present simple	Present continuous	Present perfect simple	Present perfect continuous

   a) Plastic is made from oil.

   b) She has just made a beautiful cake.

   c) They have been playing cards for two hours.

   d) They are living in Lyon till they find a new job.

   e) They have gone looking for mushrooms to pick.

   f) The chairs are made of metal, not plastic.

   g) They are walking now and then going for a swim later.

   h) It has rained every day since we've been here.

   i) The cat has been sleeping in the shade because it is so hot.

   j) The police have just finished searching the house for clues.

2 Look at the pictures below and on pages 47 and 48. Write a sentence about each one, using the present form given.

   a)

Present simple

   b)

Present simple

c)

_____

_____

Present perfect simple

d)

_____

_____

Present perfect simple

e)

BUS
STOP

_____

_____

Present continuous

f)

_____

_____

Present continuous

g)

_____

_____

Present perfect continuous

h)

_____

_____

Present perfect continuous

3 Read the following paragraph about Danae and complete the sentences about what she says.

I'll just talk about what I normally do in a week – I'm sure it's pretty much the same as many other kids around the world, because we all do roughly the same things, although maybe in different ways.

Well, here in Cyprus I suppose we have it quite easy. The school day lasts from 07.40 until 13.45 every day, and there is no school at the weekends. Kids have been going to primary and secondary school now for at least 45 years. The afternoons are free but of course we don't just sit around doing nothing! We do our homework, go for extra lessons or, if we're lucky, go out and play.

In the afternoon on Tuesdays and Fridays I go to my dance lessons, which are great – I am learning classical ballet and modern dance. Apart from dance I don't do any sport in the afternoons because I don't particularly enjoy it. I might do some extra physics lessons with my dad, who is a teacher, but because he's away at the moment I've had to miss those.

We've got some hens that we keep in a run in our garden. Because my dad is away now I have to feed them every day – but I don't mind because they're really funny to watch! That's where I've just been – I collected five eggs today!

a) On Saturdays ——————————————————————————.

b) Today ——————————————————————————————.

c) At the moment ————————————————————————.

d) I have just ————————————————————————————.

e) Always ————————————————————————————————.

f) I haven't been ————————————————————————.

g) Nowadays ——————————————————————————————.

h) Never ——————————————————————————————————.

i) Since ————————————————————————————————————.

j) I usually ——————————————————————————————.

4 Find an example of each of the following in the text on page 48. Make sure you give a different answer for each part.

a) Something that Danae does all the time.

b) Something that she is only doing now.

c) Something she enjoys doing.

d) Something she doesn't enjoy doing.

e) Something she does for someone or something else.

f) Something she only does on certain days.

g) Something all children in Cyprus do.

h) Something she does twice a week.

i) Something only some children do.

j) Something her father does.

Skills

1 Match the following words to their meanings.

league	attack
valley	the name of a group of soldiers
Light Brigade	a measurement of length
dismay'd	question
blunder'd	messed up
reason	area between two mountains
charge	disappointed or sad

2 Here are the first two verses of the poem *The Charge of the Light Brigade*. The words in Exercise 1 are missing. Put them in the correct places.

The Charge of the Light Brigade

Half a _____ , half a league,
Half a league onward,
All in the valley of Death.
Rode the six hundred.
'Forward, the Light Brigade!
_____ for the guns!' he said;
Into the _____ of Death.
Rode the six hundred.

'Forward, the _____ !'
Was there a man _____ ?
Not tho' the soldier knew
Some one had _____ ;
Theirs not to make reply,
Theirs not to _____ why,
Theirs but to do and die;
Into the valley of Death
Rode the six hundred.

by Alfred Tennyson, 9 December 1854

---

3 Answer the following questions about the poem.

a) How far did the soldiers have to go?

b) Where were they riding to?

c) Why was it called 'The Valley of Death'?

d) How many soldiers were there in the Light Brigade?

e) Who do you think said 'Charge for the guns!'

f) What do you think happened to the soldiers when they 'charged for the guns'?

g) What didn't the soldiers know when they rode?

h) Do you think this poem could happen today? Why/why not?

i) What is the poem telling us about soldiers?

j) Do you agree with what the poem is saying?

4 Think about the life of a soldier today and the life of a soldier in 1854. What do you think are the differences and the similarities? Make a list of your ideas, then write some sentences using the comparison and contrast language you have learnt in this unit.

Similarities

_____

_____

_____

_____

_____

Differences

_____

_____

_____

_____

_____

Unit 8   TV and cinema

Vocabulary

1 You need to look at Unit 8 of your Coursebook to complete this exercise. Find the answers to the following questions:

a) How many films are listed in Section A Exercise 1 (page 90)?

b) One of the films listed features hobbits, dwarves and elves. What other characters are in it?

c) In what year did people sit down to watch the first motion picture?

d) What's wrong with this name: D2-R2?

e) What is the title of the reading text in Section B?

f) What is 'propaganda'?

g) How old are young adults?

h) How many different programmes are listed in the listening text?

i) Which is better: 'All kids are asked to attend the meeting' or 'All children are asked to attend the meeting'? Why?

j) What character is named in the grammar section?

k) How many past forms are practised?

l) What is the name of the quiz show mentioned in the Let's write section?

m) What is the first word to learn in the spelling section?

n) How many TV sets are there in China?

o) What happened in 1975?

2 There are **15** words from Unit 8 in the word snake on page 53: what are they? Find them and then use the words to complete the crossword.

- a thing on which people watch programmes
- a place where people go to watch films
- a word to describe what people watch or do to enjoy themselves
- a person who works in films and takes on a different character
- made of paper, this contains a story
- we read the daily news in these
- this can be used to influence a person's thoughts and ideas
- a word to describe all the ways of giving out information
- a study of a factual story
- the correct or expected way to do something

- liked by many people
- a character that is drawn and not real
- made
- convincing or influential
- something we watch or plan

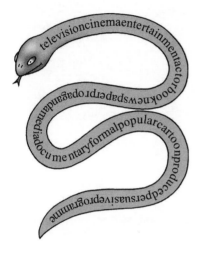

3 The letters of each word have been mixed up. Put them in their correct order and write the word next to its meaning.

a) e n y o l l   _____   feeling alone

b) s l o j a e u   _____   protective of your possessions/achievements

c) l d t r n i u i s a   _____   to do with factories

d) u e s s i   _____   the subject or matter

e) g k w d l o n e e   _____   information or understanding

f) r i s t g n e e n t i   _____   attractive or exciting

g) n i s n e l i g t   _____   hearing

h) i p r u t n e r t   _____   stop someone

4 Find the **15** pairs of names and phrases to do with films. For example:

Bilbo Baggins

R2	Harry	Daniel	Legolas
Orlando	~~Bilbo~~	MetroGoldwyn	Star
full	Mickey	soap	Walt
Rudolf	Extra	opera	Disney
D2	Radcliffe	Jungle	Mouse
Terrestrial	Greenleaf	Mayer	length
~~Baggins~~	Bloom	Valentino	Wars
Potter	Darth	Book	Vader

Grammar

Past simple	Past continuous	Past perfect simple	Past perfect continuous

1 Put each of the following sentences into the correct box.

a) The farmers rose early in the morning to feed the sheep.

b) They had been going to karate for two years, but then they stopped.

c) They were walking down the country lane when they saw an injured fox.

d) I had to give up my ballet classes because I had no time for them.

e) They had to learn to drive because the public transport was so bad.

f) The whole village was burnt down so they had to rebuild it.

g) It had been raining for two days before they decided to leave.

h) A lot of war films were produced at a time when many people were against war.

i) They were making the Harry Potter films when the actor who played Dumbledore died.

j) The film *The Sound of Music* was based on a true story of an Austrian family.

2 Look at the pictures below and on page 56 and write a sentence about each one, using the past form given.

a)

Past simple

_____

_____

b)

Past simple

_____

_____

c)

Past perfect simple

_____

_____

d)

Past perfect simple

e)

_____

_____

Past continuous

f)

_____

_____

Past continuous

g)

_____

_____

Past perfect continuous

h)

_____

_____

1997–2006   2006–Now

Past perfect continuous

3 Complete the sentences on page 57 using the verbs given. You will
need to make changes to the verbs so that the sentences are in the
past tense.

| appear | draw | watch | rise | get | make |
| produce | show | start | is | is | is |

a) The first film _____ in 1895.

b) The first films _____ silent.

c) While people _____ the film, someone would play a piano.

d) They _____ making films when they developed sound.

e) The film industry _____ stronger when World War II started.

f) The pictures on televisions _____ black and white.

g) The number of people going to the cinema _____ when television became popular.

h) Rudolph Valentino _____ a famous early actor.

i) Cartoons first _____ at the cinema about 100 years ago.

j) Walt Disney _____ many films before he died.

k) Mickey Mouse had already been created when *Snow White* _____

l) Cartoons were _____ by hand before computer technology was developed.

4 How many marks can you get? Complete the table, then use your dictionary to check your answers – score 1 mark for each correct verb.

Verbs	Past simple	Past continuous	Past perfect	Past perfect continuous
to be				
to have				
to go				
to hear				
to invite				
to learn				
to smile				
to buy				
to think				
to catch				

Total marks: _____/40

Skills

1 How much do you know about the television series *Lost*? Is it shown in your country?

Here is some information about it. Match the questions with the answers.

Questions	Answers
Which country was it made in?	English
Where was it mostly filmed?	45 minutes
When was the first series shown?	No, it was one of the most expensive on TV
What is the main storyline?	ABC
What kind of series is it?	No, it has become an international series
What is the language of the series?	Damon Lindelof
How long is each episode?	America
Which television channel was it shown on?	16 million
Who was one of the creators of the series?	About some plane crash survivors
About how many viewers were there originally?	2004
Was the series cheap to make?	Drama
Is it only shown in America?	In Hawaii

2 Read the text about *Lost*, then decide whether the statements that follow on page 59 are true or false.

Lost is an American drama television series that follows the lives of a group of plane crash survivors on a mysterious tropical island, after a commercial passenger jet flying between Sydney, Australia, and Los Angeles, United States, crashes somewhere in the South Pacific. The pilot episode was first broadcast in 2004 and since then four series have been aired. Because of its large cast and the cost of filming in Hawaii, the series is one of the most expensive on television.

Critically acclaimed and a popular success, Lost had an average of 16 million viewers per episode during the first year and has won numerous awards. The show has become part of American popular culture, with references to the story appearing in other television shows, commercials, comic books, etc.

a) The South Pacific is a tropical island.

b) Sydney, Australia, is in the United States.

c) The pilot referred to is the pilot of the aeroplane.

d) Hawaii is a very expensive place to film in.

e) A total of 16 million people have seen the series.

f) It has won many prizes.

g) *Lost* has become more than just a series.

h) It is very popular in America.

3 Imagine that you have been asked to advertise the new series of *Lost*. Use the ideas in the Let's write section of your Coursebook (page 99) to help you prepare an advertisement.

Unit 9 — The internet

Vocabulary

1 How many words can you think of to do with the internet? Complete the spider diagram below with at least **20** words.

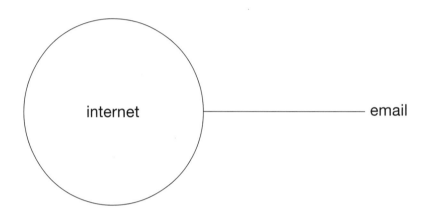

internet — email

2 Now find **12** words in the wordsearch that are to do with the internet.

V	W	N	N	I	T	E	E	S	C	L	F
I	O	W	O	R	M	S	R	E	Y	I	I
R	R	W	P	A	O	E	G	L	B	A	R
T	L	S	O	F	T	W	A	R	E	M	E
U	D	H	A	C	K	E	R	S	R	E	W
A	W	N	C	P	K	R	P	H	S	S	A
L	I	D	R	O	W	S	S	A	P	P	L
G	D	N	O	V	S	N	Q	N	A	A	L
A	E	T	I	E	F	E	A	T	C	M	N
M	W	T	C	Y	B	E	R	M	E	N	F
E	E	V	I	R	U	S	R	B	R	N	T
S	B	U	H	G	Y	Y	R	A	O	W	D

3 There is **one** mistake in each of the following sentences. Find the mistake and correct it.

a) The Japanese developed a postal system to deliver written messages in 900 BC.

b) Pigeons carried messages about the Olympic Games for the Romans in 776 BC.

c) Byzantine ships used fire to send signals to one another across the water in 900 AD.

d) Early newspapers were published in England in the 17th century.

e) The first computer program was advertised in the 1830s.

f) Samuel Morse invented a telegraph that sent short and long messages in 1837.

g) Google was invented in 1876.

h) The first short-distance phone calls were made in 1884.

i) The first radio signal was sent across the Pacific Ocean in 1901.

j) Pictures were first sent over telegraph lines in 1924.

k) The first communication satellite was launched allowing for worldwide viewing of the Winter Olympics in 1963.

l) The internet was invented by the US government for military attacks in 1970.

m) The first text messages were sent in 1972.

n) The personal music system was developed in 1975.

o) The World Wide Web was destroyed in 1990.

p) The first browser program was created allowing people to find their way around emails in 1993.

4 The letters of each word have been mixed up. Put them in their correct order and write the word next to its meaning.

a) d r n m o e _____ present day

b) n s s u a e e l m o c i l _____ various or mixed

c) o m e e v o r r _____ furthermore or in addition

d) r l m i e a a t _____ fabric or information

e) r g r a e m a i _____ wedding

f) f h i m i e c s _____ naughtiness

g) w i m h n e e l a _____ for now

h) y e l l v o _____ very nice

5 Look at these words. Match them to their meanings.

ate	the opposite of 'yes'
eight	the opposite of 'day'
right	rides a horse, a king's soldier
write	land surrounded by water
night	I will
knight	money
isle	opposite of 'left'
aisle	what we did with food
I'll	the smell of something
no	to be familiar with someone or thing
know	something you do with a pen and paper
sent	a number
cent	caused somebody or something to go
scent	like a corridor

Grammar

1 Put the sentences below into the correct box. There are **two** for each one.

Future simple (will)	Be going to	Future continuous	Future perfect	Future perfect continuous	Present continuous (future meaning)	Present simple (future meaning)

a) The train arrives at 10 o'clock.

b) I'll have finished it by midnight.

c) Sara will do the washing.

d) I'll be having my lunch at that time.

e) By September they'll have been working together for three months.

f) The match begins at 15.00.

g) The President is arriving on Monday.

h) Emily will open the window.

i) I'm going to Paris tomorrow.

j) She's going to meet me outside the cinema.

k) I'll be meeting her at six tomorrow.

l) I won't have been to the gym by that time.

m) By midnight they'll have been sitting there for six hours.

n) The players are meeting after the match.

2 Look at the pictures below and on pages 64 to 66 and write a sentence about each one, using the present form given.

a)

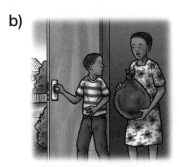

_____

_____

Future simple (will)

b)

_____

_____

Future simple (will)

c)

_____

_____

Be going to

d)

_____

_____

Be going to

e)

Future continuous

f)

Future continuous

g)

Future perfect

h)

Future perfect

i)

_____

_____

Future perfect continuous

j)

_____

_____

Future perfect continuous

k)

_____

_____

Present continuous (future meaning)

l)

_____

_____

Present continuous (future meaning)

m)

_____

_____

Present simple (future meaning)

n)

_____

_____

Present simple (future meaning)

Skills

1 Prepare a speech on the topic:

> The internet and my future

Write about 250 words. Use the Let's write section in your Coursebook (page 110) to help you.

2 Look at the following information about the internet. Rewrite it as a paragraph so that it is more interesting than just a list of facts. Add some information of your own as well.

- The internet is a global system of interconnected computer networks.
- The internet carries various information and services, such as electronic mail, online chat and other resources of the World Wide Web (WWW).
- The terms 'internet' and 'World Wide Web' do not mean the same.
- The Web is one of the services communicated by the internet.
- The internet had existed for about a decade before the WWW was available to the public.
- The Web was invented by an English scientist called Tim Berners-Lee in 1989.
- Once the internet was made available to the public, it was estimated that it grew by 100% per year.

Unit 10 Natural resources

Skills

Look at the maps of the United States of America and Indonesia and answer the questions on pages 68 to 70.

- Renewable resources: hydroelectric, biomass (plant) and wind, solar, etc.
- Non-renewable: oil and gas
- Oil consumption: 8076.0 kg per person yearly

- Population size: 276 219 000
- Area: 9 363 520 sq km
- People per sq km: 29
- Death rate: 8 per 1000 people

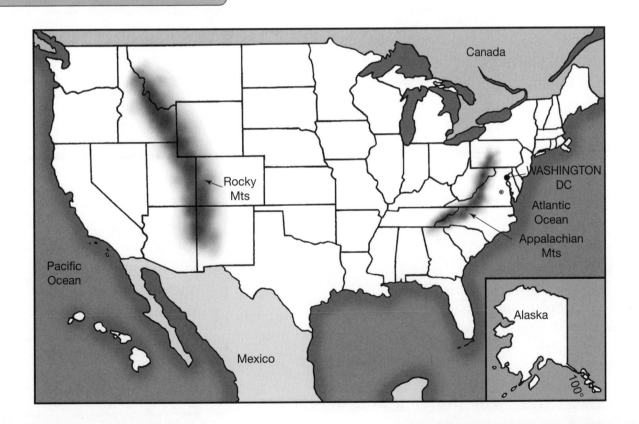

- Life expectancy: 77 years
- Literacy: 99%
- Infant mortality rate: 7 per 1000
- GDP per capita: $41 000

- Water consumption: 300 litres per day
- 90% supply of water from groundwater

- Renewable resources: solar, hydroelectric, geothermal (volcanic)
- Non-renewable: oil and gas
- Oil consumption: 693.0 kg per person yearly

- Population size: 209 205 000
- Area: 1 889 700 sq km
- People per sq km: 111
- Death rate: 7 per 1000 people

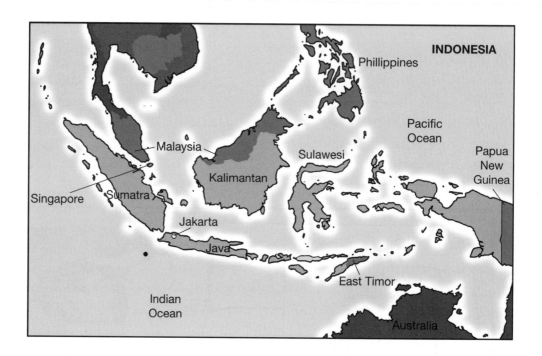

- Life expectancy: 65 years
- Literacy: 84%
- Infant mortality rate: 40 per 1000
- GDP per capita: $3600
- Water consumption: 10 litres per day

- Over 100 million lack access to safe water
- 70% of population obtain water from contaminated sources
- No national water or sanitation companies

The United States of America

a) What renewable resources are available?

_____

b) What non-renewable resources are used?

_____

c) Would you say the USA was overpopulated or underpopulated? Why? Give reasons for your answer.

_____

d) What is the death rate?

_____

e) What is an average person's life expectancy?

_____

f) What percentage of the country's population is literate?

_____

g) What is the country's infant mortality rate?

_____

h) Would you say that the USA's GDP is high or low? Give reasons for your answer.

_____

i) Roughly how much water is used by a person each day?

_____

j) Where does the USA find most of its water for public consumption?

_____

k) Would you say that the east cost of America has the same water issues as the west coast? Why?

_____

l) Which countries neighbour the USA?

_____

m) What is the capital of the USA?

_____

n) Where is the capital of the USA?

_____

o) What seas are round the USA?

_____

Indonesia

a) What renewable resources are available?

_____

b) What non-renewable resources are used?

_____

c) Does Indonesia use more or less oil than the USA?

_____

d) Would you say Indonesia was overpopulated or underpopulated? Why? Give reasons for your answer.

_____

e) What is the death rate?

_____

f) What is an average person's life expectancy?

_____

g) What percentage of the country's population is literate?

_____

h) What is the country's infant mortality rate?

_____

i) Would you say that people's GDP is high or low? Give reasons for your answer.

_____

j) Roughly how much water is used by a person each day?

_____

k) Where does Indonesia find most of its water for public consumption?

_____

l) Which countries are neighbours to Indonesia?

_____

m) What is the capital of Indonesia?

_____

n) Where is the capital of Indonesia (island and geographical location)?

_____

o) What seas are round Indonesia?

_____

Vocabulary and grammar

1 Now write some sentences comparing and contrasting the United States of America and Indonesia. Use the following words:

a) and

_____

b) but

_____

c) in the same way

_____

d) nevertheless

_____

e) similarly

_____

f) although

_____

2 You are going to write a newspaper story. Use the Let's write section in your Coursebook (page 124) to help you. Your story can be about anything you want that is connected to the topic of 'People and resources'.

You must use **five** verbs with prepositions in your story. For example, you could use these:

- laugh about
- talk to
- pay for
- look after
- without using

Or, if you prefer, you can choose **five** different verbs from the Let's do some grammar section of your Coursebook (page 121).

Unit 11 Oil

Vocabulary

1 Do the crossword. The words are all connected to the subject of oil.

Across

4 a word which also means oil, fuel, gasoline, etc.

6 a process that improves a product

9 make a hole downwards into the earth

11 the taking of products from one place to another

12 a place to keep something for an extended time

14 large ships that carry liquid

15 a long tube that carries liquids

Down

1 the earth is getting hotter

2 statistical characteristic of a population

3 a gas that comes out the back of cars and does damage to the environment

4 things in the atmosphere that are poisonous

5 this forms on the surface of water when oil is spilt

7 a noun which means to search

8 an adjective which means something that can be maintained or continued

10 very clean

13 a structure on land or in the sea that removes oil from the earth

2 Here are the same words in a word snake. Did you find them all?

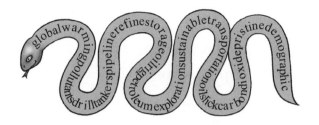

Skills

Look at the statistics about oil and answer the questions on pages 74 to 75.

Oil consumption	
Country rank	**bbl/day**
1 United States	21 000 000
2 European Union	20 800 000
3 China	6 930 000
4 Japan	5 353 000
5 Russia	2 916 000
6 India	2 438 000
7 Canada	2 290 000
8 Indonesia	1 100 000
9 Egypt	635 000
10 Jamaica	72 000

Oil production	
Country rank	**bbl/day**
1 Saudi Arabia	11 000 000
2 Russia	9 870 000
3 United States	8 322 000
4 Iran	4 150 000
5 Mexico	3 784 000
6 China	3 730 000
7 Canada	3 092 000
8 Norway	2 978 000
9 Venezuela	2 802 000
10 Kuwait	2 669 000

Oil exports	
Country rank	**bbl/day**
1 Saudi Arabia	8 900 000
2 Russia	5 080 000
3 United Arab Emirates	2 540 000
4 Iran	2 520 000
5 Norway	2 500 000
6 Canada	2 274 000
7 Mexico	2 268 000
8 Venezuela	2 203 000
9 Kuwait	2 200 000
10 Nigeria	2 141 000

Oil imports	
Country rank	**bbl/day**
1 United States	13 150 000
2 Japan	5 420 000
3 China	3 190 000
4 Germany	2 963 000
5 Netherlands	2 466 000
6 South Korea	2 410 000
7 Italy	2 182 000
8 India	2 098 000
9 France	1 890 000
10 Singapore	1 830 000

bbl/day = barrels per day

1 In your own words, explain what each of the following words mean.
   a) import
   b) export
   c) consumption
   d) production

2 Look at the countries in the tables on page 73 and list them according to which continent they are in:
   a) The Americas
   b) Asia
   c) Africa
   d) Europe

3 What do the following terms mean?
   a) country rank
   b) barrels per day

4 Use the information in the tables to answer these questions.
   a) Which country consumes more oil than any other country?

   _____

   b) What are the **two** ways in which the United States supplies itself with oil?

   _____

   c) How much oil does Venezuela keep for home use?

   _____

   d) Which **two** countries are the largest producers of oil?

   _____

   e) Which **two** countries export a very high percentage of what they produce?

   _____

   f) What does this suggest about the two countries?

   _____

   g) Nigeria exports 2 141 000 bbl/day. Talk about how this would help the economy of Nigeria.

   _____

   h) Indonesia, Egypt and Jamaica all consume a lot of oil. Talk about the negative impact this would have on their economies.

   _____

i) The Netherlands has a small and healthy economy but it imports a lot of oil. Talk about the dangers that small countries like the Netherlands might face in the future.

_____

j) Talk about where your country would appear in the tables above. Does it produce, export or import oil? Where do you think your country would rank in the table for oil consumption? Why?

_____

k) Looking at the statistics, what advantage do you think Norway has? Why?

_____

l) Look at the statistics about Canada? What do they tell you?

_____

m) According to the statistics, which two countries do not export any of the oil they produce? Why do you think this is?

_____

5 Imagine that you collected the data for the tables on page 73 for an international company. You have been asked to write how you went about finding the statistics. Where might you have found the data? Write the process that you might have used using language from the Let's write section in your Coursebook (page 137).

Grammar

1 Use the following words to make sentences/questions/suggestions, etc. connected to the tables on page 73. Use the Let's do some grammar section of your Coursebook (page 135) to help you. For example:

> do – <u>Does</u> the United States consume more oil than it produces?

> do   be   have   would   should   could   ought to   don't have to   will

2 Use the words in the box to complete the paragraph about the tables on page 73.

> may   might   will   would   should   can   could   must   ought to
> don't have to

The United States of America is one of the largest world consumers of oil. This trend _____ continue in the future, although many countries have advised the USA that it _____ reduce the amount of oil it uses. Whether this _____ happen is uncertain because many Americans don't think about how much oil they actually use compared to people in other countries. Some people in America _____ listen to the need to decrease the amount of oil used, but they are a minority. The pressure to reduce the amount of oil used _____ come from abroad – other countries _____ force the United States to become more careful and aware of their oil use. This _____ be very difficult to do, since Americans _____ do it if they don't want to. Of course, they _____ be forced to do it, if the oil actually runs out – we know that this really _____ happen!

Unit 12 Resource management

Vocabulary

Use the words in the box to complete the sentences below and on page 78. You may need to change the words slightly.

> Mediterranean   desert   overconsumption   desertification   recycle
> overpopulation   derivative   conjunctions   questionnaire   priorities
> queue   process   preparation   generations   income   desalination
> peninsula   reservoir   reduce   developing

a) There was a long _____ of people waiting to buy tickets at the cinema.

b) They have _____ the amount of water they use each month to about half.

c) Italy, Greece and Cyrus are countries in the _____

d) Many jobs are badly paid and the people receive a low _____.

e) Lovely is a _____ of love.

f) _____ plants are not a good way of supplying water because they use so much oil.

g) 'And' and 'but' are two _____ which are used regularly in English.

h) A lot of _____ was put into making the party successful so I hope lots of people turn up.

i) Camels are used in the _____ because they can travel long distances without water.

j) The _____ of making a cake can be quite simple, if you do it correctly.

k) There is a drought in Cyprus and for the first time ever the _____ are empty.

l) _____ of families have been going to the same restaurant and now they are thinking of closing it down!

m) The _____ world is increasing the amount of oil it uses, making it a more valuable commodity.

n) The present _____ of the world's natural resources will create problems for people of the future.

o) The _____ of many countries is the result of a decrease in the amount of rain falling over recent years.

p) Pupils at the school were asked to complete a _____ giving their opinions about the subjects they study.

q) A piece of land which juts into the sea is called a _____

r) Many countries in Europe now _____ their paper, plastics and glass.

s) The _____ of land reduces the amount of space for wildlife.

t) Different people have different _____

Grammar

1 Explain how you know that the subject and verb agreement in each of the following sentences is correct. Write **three** sentences about each of them.

a) The children and the teachers were very excited about the school trip.

b) All their luggage was lost when they travelled.

c) She will enjoy the theatre because she has never been before.

2 There are **ten** mistakes in the following passage. Find and correct them.

Saving water are a problem for many people because they do not understand how to do it. This is the fault of governments and the education system – not only is people not told what they could do in order to save water, but also they were not made to understand why they should save water.

It is in fact quite an easy thing to do because very often people use much more water than they need to. This means that they only need to adopt simple practice in the home and at work in order to see the amount of water they use every day decreasing quite significant.

Unfortunately, in the developed world, people are not encouraged to save water – if anything, they are encouraged to waste more. For example, many people now have power showers'. That use more water because the higher 'power' means that more water is pushed through the sprays. Another example was people wanting green lawns and swimming pools in their gardens because it looks nicer and more fashion. This wastes a lot of water and should be discouraged, especially in countries where water are a serious problem.

Skills

Urban competitiveness

New York is the world's most competitive city, according to a study. The study ranks 500 cities on their ability to attract and use resources to generate wealth. The cities are assessed on nine measures, including income, economic growth, innovation, jobs, prices and the presence of multinational firms. The report found that the gap between the best performing cities and the worst is widening. Indeed, there is a fairly large gap between the top two cities, New York and London, and Tokyo in third place. Cities in Europe and North America are richest, but China has the fastest growing ones. Asian cities also score highly in attracting multicultural companies.

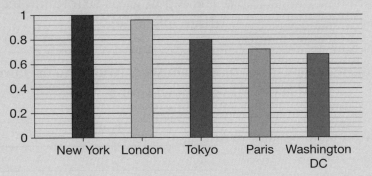

1 Use the text above to help you match the following words to their meanings.

urban	companies, businesses
competitive	international, global
ranks	money earned every month
assessed	in the city or built up areas
generate	places or numbers as
income	make or produce
innovation	ready for action and competition
multinational	be a focus for or invite
firms	new ideas
attract	measured

2 Answer the questions below and on page 80 by writing sentences.

a) According to the graph, which is the most successful city?

_____

b) In which five countries would you find each of the **five** cities mentioned?

_____

_____

_____

c) In your own words describe what the graph shows.

_____

_____

d) How many cities did the total report look at?

_____

e) What **two** verbs describe what a city does with its resources, in order to generate wealth?

_____

f) The report gives six of nine measures. What do you think the other **three** might be?

_____

g) Explain what 'widening' is. Give **two** reasons why you think the gap is widening.

_____

_____

_____

h) The report says 'but China has the fastest growing ones'. What does 'ones' refer to? Can you name **two**?

_____

_____

i) Name **three** other cities in Europe that might be among the richest, as mentioned in the report. Say why you chose those three cities.

_____

_____

_____

j) Why do you think it is important for a city to attract multinational companies? What resources do you think a multinational company would bring to a city?

_____

_____

3 Imagine that you have been asked to suggest ideas on how to use the resources where you live to generate wealth for your region and its people. Write a report of about 200 words. Give clear reasons for your suggestions.

Unit 13 Intelligence

Vocabulary

1 Write all the letters of the alphabet

1	2	3	4	5	6	7	8	9	10	11	12	13
a	b	c	___	___	___	___	___	___	___	___	___	___

14	15	16	17	18	19	20	21	22	23	24	25	26
___	___	___	___	___	___	___	___	___	___	___	___	___

Now work out what these words are, using the code.

a) 9 14 20 5 12 12 9 7 5 14 3 5   _____

b) 9 14 20 5 18 16 5 18 19 15 14 1 12   _____

c) 19 16 1 20 9 1 12   _____

d) 20 8 5   3 15 14 4 9 20 9 15 14 1 12   _____

e) 2 9 15 7 18 1 16 8 9 5 19   _____

f) 7 5 18 13 1 14 25   _____

g) 18 5 3 5 9 22 5   _____

h) 16 5 5 18   _____

i) 19 1 20 21 18 4 1 25   _____

j) 15 3 20 1 7 15 14   _____

2 The writer of the following passage has chosen **12** words wrongly. Find them and change the words to the correct ones.

One day I was looking through some magazines at pictures of the dessert, and thinking how quite and peaceful it must be their, and imagining the different sents of the sand, when I herd a noise outside the house. I looked at the seen outside but all seemed quite stationery and normal. The only movement I could sea was the woman next door, whose got a lovely garden – she was working in it. I saw that she was holding a peace of would in her hand, witch looked like it had fallen from a tree.

3 Write a meaningful sentence for each of the following groups of words. You must use all the words given, but they can be in any order you wish and you can add your own words. For example:

> read, study, ability, sandwich, listening
> The <u>ability</u> to <u>read</u> and <u>study</u> is no problem but when it comes to <u>listening</u> she has to eat a <u>sandwich</u> at the same time.

a) singing, activities, phone, man, removed

_____

_____

b) take, care, hospitalised, recently, poison, friend

_____

_____

c) music, read, doing, parrot, job

_____

_____

d) confusing, musical, comments, researching, invitation

_____

_____

Grammar

1 Complete the sentences with your own ideas.

a) If Howard Gardner hadn't suggested the idea of multiple intelligences _____.

b) If there weren't eight different intelligences _____.

c) If Robin Hood had been a real man _____.

d) If parrots could really talk _____.

e) If the subjects taught at school were changed _____.

2 Write **ten** sentences about the picture, in the conditional. For example:

> If the man had arrived earlier, he wouldn't have missed his train.

3 Look at the pictures and write a conditional sentence about each one. Use the example to help you.

If a horse didn't have such long and strong legs, it wouldn't be able to run so fast.

a)

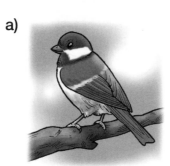

_____

_____

b)

_____

_____

c)

_____

_____

d)

_____

_____

Skills

1 Match the sentences to build a biography of the scientist Marie Curie.

She lived from …	doctorate she met her husband, Pierre Curie.
She grew up in …	Nobel laureates and scientists.
She was a …	leukaemia – a cancer of the blood.
She was the first woman to receive …	1867 to 1934.
She had a great aptitude for …	a street accident by a wayward cart-horse.
When she was young it was …	scientists after Einstein.
When she was studying for her …	aware of the dangers of their discoveries.
Together they discovered …	had been working with all her life finally killed her.
Neither she or her husband were …	radium.
Her husband was killed in …	after his death.
She continued with her research …	physics and mathematics.
She was one of the most famous …	physicist and chemist.
The dangerous materials that she …	the Nobel Prize for Physics and to teach at the University of Paris.
She died of …	illegal for girls to study in higher education.
Their children went on to become …	Russian-dominated Poland.

2 Use the following notes to write a biography about Bill Gates, the famous founder of Microsoft.

- 1955–the present day
- born and lives in Seattle, Washington USA
- born into wealthy family
- father a prominent lawyer
- was a brilliant pupil, especially gifted at mathematics
- first introduced to computers in early teens
- formed first company at 16 years old
- Microsoft formed 1975
- company grew hugely 1980s
- married 1994, three children
- retired from Microsoft when still a young man
- is one of best-known entrepreneurs of the personal computer revolution
- donates large amounts of money to various charitable organisations and scientific research programmes

The human brain

Vocabulary

1 Read the following sentences and decide whether an American person or a British person is speaking in each case. Underline the word/s that tell you this.

a) Would you like a candy?

b) You aren't allowed to wear sneakers at school, are you?

c) There are a lot of different insects in the garden this year.

d) He bought some new pants to wear with his jacket.

e) Cars shouldn't park on the pavement because it is dangerous for pedestrians.

f) She looked very smart in her outfit.

g) The aeroplane that crashed was an old one.

h) The cinema was packed last night and we couldn't get a seat.

i) The tires of the lorry exploded and it went off the road.

j) Please put the rubbish out – the dustmen are coming now.

k) The freeways in Italy can be very narrow.

l) The leaves are a beautiful colour every fall.

2 Match the following sentences to make facts about the brain.

It weighs about …	of the colour of blood.
It feels …	complex brains.
It makes up only …	two parts.
A baby's brain increases in size …	three times in the first year.
The brain is …	1.4 kilos.
It looks pink because …	result in serious damage.
It feels like …	a ripe avocado.
Loss of blood can …	mostly water.
It is divided into …	the body's energy.
We have very …	2% of the body's weight.
It uses a large percentage of …	no pain.

3 Complete each of the sentences below and on page 88 using the phrases in the box below.

> scatter brain   an early bird   free as a bird   eats like a bird
> a little bird told me   bird brain   brain drain   brain dead
> all brawn and no brain   rack your brains

a) that you were getting married.

b) She is as and travels all over the world.

c) She is a real and has no common sense.

d) He is normally by the end of the day, he's so tired.

e) She and needs to put on more weight.

f) There has been a from British universities to American ones.

g) You must and try and think of that name!

h) He is not a very intelligent kid but he's great at football – he's .

i) She is a real and can never organise herself.

j) He has much more energy in the mornings and is a real .

Grammar

Complete the following sentences using these forms of the verbs given.

   a) present

   b) past

   c) present participle

   d) past participle

1 Verb: to begin

   a) I _____ each day with breakfast.

   b) I _____ learning English many years ago.

   c) I am _____ to enjoy reading this book.

   d) I have _____ to eat more fruit every day.

2 Verb: to fly

   a) We _____ the flag at the Olympic games.

   b) The birds _____ all the way from the African continent.

   c) They are _____ with the national carrier.

   d) She has _____ all over the world and she's only 12!

3 Verb: to draw

   a) They _____ every day, at the end of lessons.

   b) He _____ the picture for a competition.

   c) They are _____ the scenery for the play.

   d) He has _____ some very nice pictures in his art lessons.

4 Verb: to bring

   a) She _____ a sandwich to school every day.

   b) They _____ all the books in yesterday.

   c) She is _____ a cake in for all of us.

   d) They have _____ in the wrong school books.

5 Verb: to take

a) They _____ too long in getting ready every morning.

b) She _____ her bag but forgot her purse.

c) They are _____ their final exams this year.

d) It has _____ us 20 minutes to get here.

6 Verb: to buy

a) She _____ too many clothes and wastes her money.

b) They _____ a new fridge because the old one was too small.

c) They are _____ furniture slowly because it is very expensive.

d) Peter has _____ some milk so I don't need any more.

7 Verb: to speak

a) She _____ very badly and I have difficulty understanding her.

b) The headmaster _____ for a whole hour on school discipline.

c) She is _____ on the telephone, so please wait a minute.

d) Alex has _____ about this for months now.

8 Verb: to lay

a) A waitress must know how to _____ a table correctly.

b) She _____ the books out tidily on the table.

c) They are _____ the clean sheets on the bed.

d) The chicken has _____ two eggs this morning.

9 Verb: to lie

a) She _____ on the beach all day in the sun.

b) He didn't feel well yesterday so he _____ on the sofa all day.

c) They are _____ on their beds because they feel a bit tired.

d) She has _____ on that bed now for hours and I think it is time to get her up.

10 Verb: to sing

a) She _____ every week with a choir.

b) He _____ in the school choir this year which was great.

c) The children are _____ again this year.

d) They have _____ every year but don't want to this year.

Skills

1 Read the text below, then decide whether the statements that follow are true or false.

Who was Neanderthal man?

In the hope of learning how humans developed, scientists study whatever remains of prehistoric man they can find. These include tools, cooking utensils, skeletons, and parts of the body.

In 1856, the remains of men were dug from a limestone cave in the Neander Gorge in Germany. These were the first complete skeletons ever found of prehistoric man, and they had survived because these people buried their dead.

Neanderthal people probably lived in central Asia, the Middle East and many parts of Europe, from about 150 000 to about 30 000 years ago – a period of about 120 000 years.

What was Neanderthal man like? He was heavy and stocky. His skull was flat. His face was long with a heavy jaw. He did not have much chin or forehead. Probably the earliest Neanderthal people lived when the climate was warm, between glacial periods. But then another ice age came and they began to live in caves and learnt how to fight the cold.

There are many hearths in the caves that have been found, showing that these people used fire to keep warm and protect themselves. They also may have cooked their meat.

Neanderthal man not only had hand axes, they also had 'flake' tools. These are tools that were made of broad, thin flakes of flint with a good, sharp edge.

Some of the flake tools were points in the shape of rough triangles. They probably served as knives for skinning and cutting up animals. Neanderthal hunters may also have used pointed wooden spears.

But the most curious thing about Neanderthal man is that he had a larger brain than modern man has!

a) Skeletons were found in 1856.

b) Neanderthal people lived 70 000 years ago.

c) Neanderthal people lived only in the Neander Gorge.

d) The Neanderthal people existed for about 120 000 years.

e) The Neanderthal people were not very tall.

f) The third picture best describes the Neanderthal people.

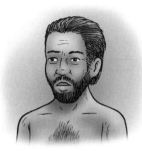

g) The climate changed while the Neanderthal man existed.

h) They originally lived in caves.

i) The Neanderthal people were used to the cold weather.

j) They learnt the skill of making fire.

k) They used tools for hunting and daily life.

l) The text suggests that Neanderthal people were more intelligent than humans.

2 Look at the picture of an 11-year-old child from 19th-century England. Imagine that you are that child. You work down a coal mine. Describe your life, using the picture to help you. Write about 200 words.

Unit 15 Animals' brains

Vocabulary

1 Find the **11** names of famous animals in the wordsearch.

```
M   N   N   G   T   I   G   G   E   R   H   5
I   E   R   A   G   N   R   T   E   E   E   9
C   V   K   R   B   U   M   N   S   S   D   1
K   O   C   F   A   M   A   M   I   Y   W   4
E   H   U   I   K   S   I   O   E   E   I   Z
Y   T   D   E   I   T   I   S   R   M   G   M
M   E   D   L   N   M   S   A   O   I   A   T
O   E   L   D   G   H   U   N   U   P   R   O
U   B   A   A   K   E   S   M   O   E   C   E
S   I   N   I   O   S   R   H   B   O   A   I
E   L   O   I   N   H   H   E   S   L   P   T
E   S   D   H   G   L   A   S   S   I   E   Y
```

2 Match the words and expressions to their meanings.

foe	This helps to makes something or someone blend in with their environment.
forebears	This describes a person who is not very brave.
innate	This person is an enemy.
adaptive	This word refers to the amount of something.
camouflage	These are only pretend and not real signs of sorrow.
copy cat	This is a person who likes to do the same as others.
black sheep	This word describes a style or way of doing something.
crocodile tears	This word describes a group of words which connect parts of a sentence.
chicken	Those who came before us.
white elephant	One who does not fit in with the normal group.
quantity	Able to change oneself in order to fit in with the environment.
conjunctions	A mother's natural instincts over her young are this.
strategy	This normally describes a waste of space.
technique	This also means a plan.

3 Answer the following 'Why' questions.

   a) Why is an elephant's brain bigger than that of other animals?

   b) Why can an owl turn its head right round?

   c) Why does a monkey live in trees?

   d) Why were pigeons useful birds?

   e) Why are bees such sweet insects?

   f) Why does an elephant never forget?

   g) Why are polar bears white?

   h) Why is a soldier like an animal?

   i) Why didn't many animals die in the tsunami?

   j) Why can't a lion see a zebra when it is standing still?

   k) Why could Harry Potter talk to snakes?

   l) Why can donkeys be dangerous?

   m) Why do most people not like rats?

4 Here are the answers to Exercise 3. Match them with the correct questions. How many did you get right?

   i) Because they live in the snow and need to blend in with their environment.

   ii) Because they kill many people in a year.

   iii) Because they make honey.

   iv) Because he could speak Parseltongue – the language of snakes.

   v) To protect itself and see if there are any dangers around it.

   vi) Because a lion is colour blind and can see only black and white.

   vii) Because it has a large body.

   viii) Because both use camouflage to protect themselves.

   ix) Because they are dirty and there are so many of them.

   x) To protect itself from the dangers on the ground.

   xi) Because they used to carry messages.

   xii) Because they have very good memories.

   xiii) Because they sensed the danger and escaped beforehand.

Grammar

1 Complete the sentences on page 94 to describe the picture. Use some of the words in the box in your sentences – you can use them more than once. You will also need to choose some other words.

> few   a few   a little   little   many   much   a lot of   lots of

For example:

> There are <u>lots of</u> zebras running about in the <u>field</u>.

a) There are also _____ flamingos in the same field as the

_____.

b) There are _____ people watching _____ monkeys in

a _____.

c) _____ of the monkeys _____ bananas.

d) There is only _____ water in the _____ bowl.

e) The people have to leave soon because there isn't _____

time left.

f) There isn't _____ space for the monkeys to _____.

g) There are only _____ giraffes in the _____.

h) Not _____ people are looking at the _____.

i) _____ people have cameras and are taking _____ of

the animals.

2 Use one of the words in the boxes below to complete the sentences.

Time	Cause and effect	Opposition	Condition
after	because	although	if
before	since	though	only if
when	now that	even though	whether or not
while	in order that	whereas	even if
since	so	while	in case

a) I will come with you _____ we can leave later.

b) We will leave _____ it is time to leave and not before.

c) _____ it is holiday time you can wake up later in the mornings.

d) They haven't been to the cinema _____ the summer.

e) You should drink more milk _____ you want to.

f) You will keep your room tidy _____ you live in this house.

g) _____ everybody doesn't arrive on time, we'll start anyway.

h) She still came late, _____ she had been told not to be.

i) The girls liked the film, _____ the boys didn't.

j) They have to come to help _____ we won't have enough people otherwise.

k) _____ they were sleeping I managed to do the housework.

l) You can have some sweets _____ you eat your dinner first.

m) _____ they walked all that way, they still had energy left.

n) You can watch television _____ you've finished your homework.

o) _____ you beg me for it, I won't get it for you.

p) He did tell me what happened, _____ I don't believe him.

q) _____ they don't do what I've asked, I've decided to do it myself.

r) They have been to the United States _____.

s) They bought a lot of them _____ they can save some money.

t) They're not allowed to watch any TV _____ they're not finishing their homework.

Skills

1 Read the poem below and on page 96.

> ### The Song of the Mischievous Dog
> There are many who say that a dog has its day,
>   And a cat has a number of lives;
> There are others who think that a lobster is pink,
>   And that bees never work in their hives.
> There are fewer, of course, who insist that a horse
>   Has a horn and two humps on its head,
> And a fellow who jests that a mare can build nests
>   Is as rare as a donkey that's red.

Yet in spite of all this, I have moments of bliss,
  For I cherish a passion for bones,
And though doubtful of biscuit, I'm willing to risk it,
  And I love to chase rabbits and stones.
But my greatest delight is to take a good bite
  At a calf that is plump and delicious;
And if I indulge in a bite at a bulge,
  Let's hope you won't think me too vicious.

Dylan Thomas

Now match the words to their meanings.

mischievous	fat, meaty
insist	extreme happiness
fellow	female horse
jests	jokes
mare	naughty
rare	nasty
bliss	spoil or make a fuss of
calf	stick to an idea
plump	young cow
indulge	not common
vicious	male person

2 Answer the following questions.

   a) Find the **eight** pairs of rhyming words in the poem.

   b) What does the poem try to tell us about animals?

   c) In your own words explain the title of the poem.

   d) There are **four** things that the dog says many people believe. What are they and what do you know about them?

   e) Name **two** animals that have a horn and/or a hump.

   f) In your own words explain what the dog is telling us about himself.

   g) Do you think we see dogs as they really are? How do you think our picture of dogs is different from how dogs see themselves?

   h) Think of **two** other things which people might believe about animals.

3 You have learnt a lot about animals in this unit. Write an essay of about 200 words entitled 'Animals'.

Vocabulary

1 Find **13** words in the wordsearch.

```
A  E  G  Y  P  T  I  A  N  A  B  H
S  T  N  E  M  N  R  E  V  O  G  E
O  E  R  U  T  L  U  C  K  A  N  R
C  H  O  P  I  T  I  E  N  H  T  I
I  R  M  M  E  N  E  C  H  E  T  T
E  W  A  D  E  R  I  R  M  A  C  A
T  E  N  S  G  E  S  W  A  L  L  G
Y  A  T  E  N  O  G  T  M  P  S  E
I  N  S  T  I  T  U  T  I  O  N  S
N  O  I  T  A  S  I  L  I  V  I  C
E  R  U  T  C  E  T  I  H  C  R  A
Y  C  A  R  C  O  M  E  D  D  S  N
```

2 Guess the meaning of the underlined words in the following sentences. Use a dictionary to help you.

a) She was a complete egoist and never considered what other people wanted.

b) He had been a philatelist now for many years and had collected stamps from all over the world.

c) She never travels abroad – she is rather xenophobic.

d) He is the antithesis of his brother and always does things differently.

e) They are very antagonistic towards each other and often argue.

f) They are quite a cosmopolitan family and have travelled to many different countries.

g) The confidential report suggests that many people will lose their jobs, but this has not yet been announced.

h) The supposition is that Peter will be the next head teacher, but nobody is sure.

i) He loves gardening and especially topiary – he has grown and shaped many bushes.

j) Many opposition parties will be standing against each other in the elections.

Grammar

1 Write the phrasal verb which is similar in meaning to each of the following:

  a) leave home _____

  b) arrive without previous notice or warning _____

  c) say something that is not true _____

  d) persuade _____

  e) search or find _____

  f) meet by chance or unexpectedly _____

  g) take or deliver something or someone by car _____

  h) talk about in detail _____

  i) be prepared for something _____

  j) leave or depart _____

  k) start or begin _____

  l) investigate _____

2 Write a sentence using each of the following phrasal verbs. You may need to use a dictionary to check their meanings.

  a) take off

  _____

  b) take to

  _____

  c) take after

  _____

  d) take for granted

  _____

  e) take over

  _____

  f) take in

  _____

  g) take on

  _____

  h) take up

  _____

Skills

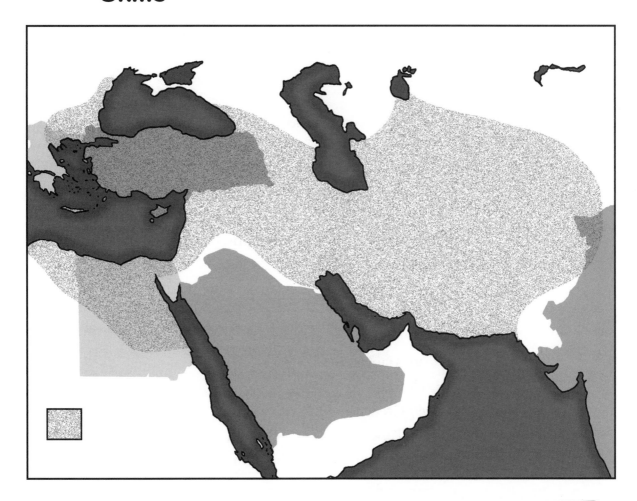

Facts about the Empire of Persia

- The Empire existed in various forms and sizes from 550 BC until 1935, when Iran was officially accepted as the name of the new country.
- The capital city of the Empire, Persepolis, was established by Darius the Great (522 to 486 BC). Its ruins are now famous.
- Tehran became the capital in 1795.
- One of the ruling families of the Persian Empire was called the Achaemenids.
- The Achaemenids held power for more than two centuries until Alexander the Great invaded and annexed the territory in 328–327 BC.
- Persian soldiers wore loose trousers which the Greeks thought were effeminate.
- The word 'pyjamas' comes from Persian and means leg (py) garment (jama).
- The so-called Royal Road ran for 2575 km from the ancient city of Susa, located in the south-east of modern-day Iran, to the west coast of what is now Turkey. The road had 100 rest stations and was considered vital for swift communication.

- *The Achaemenid kings had couriers on horseback who could travel the Royal Road in nine days to deliver oral or written messages.*
- *Farsi is the modern form of the Persian language.*
- *The Muslim religion became dominant in the 7th century but was preceded by Zoroastrianism.*
- *The skill of carpet weaving has been practised for millennia in the Persian world.*

1 Use the information above and on page 99 to help you answer the following questions. You may need to do some research for some of them.

a) Add these labels on the map:

   i) Saudi Arabia

   ii) Africa

   iii) Egypt

   iv) Mediterranean Sea

   v) Arabian Sea

   vi) India

   vii) Greece

   viii) Turkey

b) Which countries are the main neighbours of Iran?

_____

c) Name the countries which used to be part of the Persian Empire.

_____

d) Draw the route of the Royal Road on the map.

_____

e) Write **two** facts that you know about present-day Iran.

_____

_____

f) Write **two** facts that you know about the Persian Empire.

_____

_____

g) When did the Iran we know today come into existence?

_____

h) How long was Darius the Great leader of the Persian Empire?

_____

i) How long after Persepolis did Tehran become the capital?

_____

j) Who came first, Alexander the Great or the Achaemenids?

_____

k) How old was the Persian Empire when Alexander the Great came?

_____

l) What nationality was Alexander the Great?

_____

m) Which skill are the Persians internationally known for?

_____

n) Write **two** facts about your country at the time of Darius the Great.

_____

_____

o) About how long would it take to travel about 2575 km today in a car?

_____

p) Find words in the text which are similar in meaning to the following:

    i) to go before

   ii) publicly/formally

  iii) seized/took possession of

  iv) periods of 100 years

    v) womanly

  vi) clothes

 vii) fast

viii) messengers

2 Choose **one** of the titles below. Write a poem using the title of the famous book, and start each line of your poem with the words from the title.

The Lord of the Rings	Around the World in Eighty Days
The	Around
Lord	The
Of	World
The	In
Rings	Eighty
	Days

Unit 17 The world today

Vocabulary

1 Put each of the following words/expressions into the correct categories below. There are **four** for each category. Some might fit into more than one category.

> lap tops   workers' rights   urbanisation   reading and writing
> population increase   literate   UNESCO   technology   global warming
> science   pollution   factories

Industry	Environment	Education

2 Complete the paragraph using the collocations below. You may need to change the form of the verbs.

> make money   pay attention   explain why   delicate matter
> take an interest   make trouble   take a test   pay a visit   hold a meeting
> turn a blind eye   keep a straight face   fall in love   walk the dog
> take advantage   come here   pass the time

The other day I was out _____ when I thought I would _____ to my boss, who lived in the neighbourhood. I wanted to talk to him about a _____ which I did not want to discuss at work, because I thought it might _____ . I knocked on his door and when he opened it I found it hard to _____ because he looked so different from the man I was used to dealing with at work. I _____ I was there and he told me that he had _____ to the issue at work because he wanted to _____ with me about it first – so my _____ to his house was a good idea. He said he would go and make coffee

and asked me to _____ by reading a magazine, but instead I _____
of being in the room alone and had a good look around. When he came back he
_____ in what I had to say and then asked that I carefully _____ to
what he had to say. He suggested that if I want to _____ at work – which is
what I need because things are very tight financially – I should _____ that
could lead to promotion. He then told me how much he had _____ with my
dog, who had also been sitting listening to him, with her head on the side.

Grammar

Form **20** partitives using the words in the table below.

A ...	of ...
piece	trousers
box	squash
loaf	cards
bar	monopoly
packet	bread
game	research
glass	bees
tin	cake
litre	tea
bottle	matches
pair	biscuits
cup	cat food
vase	chocolate
pair	roses
drop	milk
swarm	cream
bunch	cereal
crumb	glasses
game	flowers
pack	milk

Skills

1 Here are some predictions and facts about our 21st-century society, made by some leading world figures. Read the information, then answer the questions on page 105.

Energy
Our planet, with its growing global industrialisation and population, will need energy at an increasing rate – to the point of disappearance. This will be one of the greatest challenges we will have to face in the 21st century.

Labour
Work will no longer be structured around the traditional stages of childhood, education, work and retirement. It will become part of a longer process of life-long education, with periods of rest and of social and civic activities.

Communication
The way we access information has changed so radically recently that there is no way one can understand it. First World countries have fought for a place in the digital world but it is possible that in the future the Third World won't be where we currently think it is.

Water
More than one billion people lack direct access to drinking water. It is estimated that by 2025 we will have used 70% of the Earth's renewable resources, compared to less than 50% used today.

Environment
Maybe the most significant indicator of the Earth's health is the decline of the number of species with whom we share this planet. Unfortunately, we find ourselves in the greatest process of plant and animal extinction in the last 65 million years.

a) Five topics were covered for predictions for the future. Do you think these are the most important topics? Give two more that you think are also important.

_____

_____

b) In the 'Labour' section it says: '... life-long education, with periods of rest and of social and civic activities.' Explain what this means in your own words and give examples.

_____

_____

c) Name five countries that you think don't have direct access to drinking water.

_____

d) Give two ways you think the issue of water could be dealt with in the future in countries which do not have direct access.

_____

_____

e) Give two examples of how animals and plants are becoming extinct.

_____

_____

f) Why is it a problem that animals and plants are becoming extinct?

_____

g) Read the 'Energy' opinion. Do you agree or disagree with this comment? Suggest two ways of how you might deal with it.

_____

_____

h) List two countries that are considered First World countries and list two that are considered Third World countries.

_____

_____

2 You are going to write a short drama in which two characters (played by you and a partner) are discussing an issue that you think is important in society today.

First think about what issue you would like to discuss and then plan how the script will progress.

Make sure that you use all the features of drama writing. Use the Let's write section in the Coursebook on pages 217 to 218 to help you.

Write about one A4 page.

Vocabulary

1 Decide whether the following information is true or false.

a) You can buy newspapers at a grocery.

b) The word 'guy' is a formal word used to talk about a man.

c) Gyrating could be done to music.

d) A monotonous piece of music would not be interesting.

e) If you are 'in the soup' it means you are having problems.

f) You should speak to your head teacher with deference.

g) A crumb could be from cake or bread.

h) A swot normally does well in tests and examinations.

i) A visionary person is an imaginative person.

j) A courgette and a zucchini can both be eaten.

k) Vintage wine is much more expensive than everyday wine.

l) You could carry on reading a book or carry a box on to a train.

m) If you are homesick you want to get away from home because you are sick of it.

n) Wellington boots would be no good in the rain.

o) It would be nice to sail round the world in a dinghy but not in a yacht.

2 Complete the crossword.

Across

5 protects you against disease
6 the second number
7 small insects that live
  underground
10 a form of energy
11 to do with seeing
13 places where something is
14 the beginning of something

Down

1 not noisy
2 civilisation
3 disease caused by abnormal cells
4 badly fed
8 very or also
9 learn something again, check you
  remember it
12 used on food to make moist or
  tastier

3 You can use this exercise to check the crossword in Exercise 2.

First write all the letters of the alphabet

1	2	3	4	5	6	7	8	9	10	11	12	13
a	b	c	___	___	___	___	___	___	___	___	___	___

14	15	16	17	18	19	20	21	22	23	24	25	26
___	___	___	___	___	___	___	___	___	___	___	___	___

Now work out what these words are, using the code.

a) 13 1 12 14 15 21 18 9 19 8 5 4   _____

b) 22 1 3 3 9 14 5   _____

c) 3 1 14 3 5 18   _____

d) 20 8 5 18 13 15 14 21 3 12 5 1 18   _____

e) 18 5 22 9 19 5   _____

f) 19 1 21 3 5   _____

g) 19 15 21 18 3 5   _____

h) 17 21 9 5 20   _____

i) 20 15 15   _____

j) 20 23 15   _____

k) 19 9 20 5 19   _____

l) 19 9 7 8 20 19   _____

m) 1 14 20 19   _____

n) 19 15 3 9 5 20 25   _____

Grammar

1 Complete these sentences using the verbs 'sleep' and 'drink'. Put the verbs into the tenses given.

a) Present simple

Sleep: I _____ for eight hours a night during term time.

Drink: I _____ a litre of water every day.

b) Past simple

Sleep: I _____ late in the mornings when I was on holiday.

Drink: I _____ some lovely fresh milk yesterday.

c) Present continuous

Sleep: I _____ very well at the moment.

Drink: I _____ too much coffee these days.

d) Past continuous

Sleep: I _____ on a futon because all the beds were taken.

Drink: I _____ a coffee when the doorbell rang.

e) Present perfect

Sleep: I _____ every day of my life.

Drink: I _____ enough tea today, thank you.

f) Past perfect

Sleep: I was lucky because I _____ before we got the night flight.

Drink: I felt sick because I _____ a whole litre of water.

g) Past perfect continuous

Sleep: I _____ very well before it started getting so hot.

Drink: I _____ my milk from a cup, but then my mother bought me a special glass.

h) Future simple

Sleep: I _____ on the bus – it is a very long journey.

Drink: I _____ my milk every day from now on.

i) Future perfect

Sleep: If I can lie in tomorrow morning, _____ for eight hours every night this month.

Drink: I _____ my tea by the time you are ready to go.

j) Future perfect continuous

Sleep: At lunch time he _____ for a whole day.

Drink: Next week I _____ the same type of tea for two years.

k) Future continuous

Sleep: I _____ on the couch because I said Aunt Joan can have my bed.

Drink: I _____ this evening with my dinner.

2 Write **11** sentences, one for each picture below and on pages 110 to 111, using the forms given.

a)

Present simple

b)

Past simple

c)

Present continuous

d)

Past continuous

_____

_____

e)

Present perfect

_____

_____

f)

Past perfect

_____

_____

g)

Past perfect continuous

_____

_____

h)

Future simple

_____

_____

i)

Future perfect

_____

_____

j)

Future perfect continuous

_____

_____

k)

Future continuous

_____

_____

Skills

1 Look at the picture and write a short essay of about 300 words giving your opinion about it. How realistic do you think it is? What features do you think will be true in the future, and which do you think will not? Give reasons for your ideas.

2 Thomas Jefferson, the third President of the United States of America (1801–1809), once said:

> 'I like the dreams of the future better than the history of the past.'

What do you think he meant? Do you agree or disagree with him? Give reasons for your answers.